THE
BOOK
OF
HEALING

Also by Najwa Zebian

Mind Platter
The Nectar of Pain
Sparks of Phoenix

THE BOOK OF HEALING

NAJWA ZEBIAN

Andrews McMeel
PUBLISHING®

CONTENTS

INTRODUCTION

I took my first breath the moment I started writing. That's when I started living in every nonliteral sense of the word. Writing healed me. It continues to heal me. It is the air that keeps my soul alive and the medicine that cleanses it.

Since I first published my work four years ago, I have felt more seen and heard—and less alone—than ever before. I am on a mission to accurately express my deepest emotions in words. My intention has always been to be as open, raw, and vulnerable as possible—to write about what I'm *really* experiencing on the inside. I consider this a form of self-advocacy.

I am humbled by the millions of people who have told me how they ache to give a voice to their deepest thoughts and feelings. Every person who has read my heart over the last four years has become my family. And my loved ones have sent me thousands of inquiries on themes of love, healing, and letting go. The truth is, there are many books that will tell you how you *should* heal. *The Book of Healing* is not one of those. It honors that you *are* healing—exactly as you need to be.

There is no one path to healing, but the thought patterns and emotions involved are universal. My hope is that the pieces collected here will help you put words to your own pain. While I cannot guide you through your unique process of healing, I do seek to validate what you experience. As you flip through the pages of this book, I hope you will hear my voice: "I hear you. I see you. I understand you."

I trust that reading my words will do for you what writing them did for me.

If you've been here from the beginning, thank you for walking this journey with me. And if you're new, welcome to the journey of healing.

Najwa

To the heart in you, don't be afraid to feel.
To the sun in you, don't be afraid to shine.
To the love in you, don't be afraid to heal.

To the ocean in you, don't be afraid to rage.
To the silence in you, don't be afraid to break.

Of all the gifts I could give you, I choose to give the ones I needed when I was in my darkest moments. You see, we all walk different paths, but there is one tragedy that all of us share: the struggle to be ourselves in a world that wants us to be anything but ourselves.

Here is the gift of understanding when you are in a roomful of people looking right past the pain inside of you.

Here is the gift of *me too* when you feel that you are the only one who thinks and feels the way you do.

Here is the gift of kindness when the world bundles up its heartlessness and throws it at you.

Here is the gift of love when you feel that the only love you deserve is that which others believe you are worthy of.

May these gifts light up your way when darkness overtakes your path. May these gifts allow your true self to emanate from within so that you may be your own light.

To heal from your pain
now,
you need to go all the way back
to chapter one.
To page one.
To the beginning
of how it all began.

For every ending,
there is a
once upon a time.
For every broken soul,
there is a
once upon a happy soul.
For every phoenix soaring,
there is a phoenix
burning,
turning to ashes,
rising,
then soaring.

Let me hand you the matches
to ignite the glory
within your soul.
Let me be the one
who burns to ashes
as you spark in your darkest of nights.
As you rise.
As you soar.

The world sees that
you are in pain
and says:
"Let me give you a little more.
You've handled this much.
You can handle a bit more."

CHAPTER I
FORGIVENESS

Forgive and Forget

It amazes me how we always remember how others have wronged us, but we forget how we've wronged others. We always tell ourselves to forgive but never forget. Here is my philosophy: If you want others to forgive you for what you have done wrong to them, then you should do the same. Some people need a second chance. Some people need to forgive themselves for wronging themselves and others. You can be in either situation. We need to help others and ourselves by forgiving others and, yes, by forgetting the actions that they've done as individuals. When you say *never forget,* it shouldn't mean that you will never forget the person doing the mistake but that you will never forget the mistake that was done so that you will remember how it made you feel and never do it to someone else. We are all humans. We all make mistakes. Whether we are courageous and sincere enough to admit that is a different story. If you want a second chance at being the person who you want to be, then give that chance to others. Forgive people, and forget that they have made certain mistakes, but never forget the lessons that you learned from the mistakes they made.

Be Considerate

Be considerate of others before you expect them to be considerate of you. Don't freeze time and isolate events in the desire to give yourself the right to blame others for not treating you with whatever you define as *right*. In the grand scheme of things, it is probably your perception that needs to change. Think before you speak, and reap what you sow. Don't ever seek refuge only in people, for if you do, they will fail you sooner or later. But if you seek refuge in and forgiveness from a power much greater than yourself, you will not be turned away, and your eyes will be opened to the *right* right.

Inspire

If you aim for perfect, you will always be disappointed. Don't expect everyone to be up to your expectations unless you are willing to live up to someone else's. We have to accept that no one is perfect and learn to let go of the mentality that people can't change. People are not all born into the same environment, and they are not born with the same definition of what is right and what is wrong. What we see as someone making a mistake may only be our perception that something is wrong. Their perception may be that everything is completely fine. Sometimes all a person needs is to fall once or twice to learn on his or her own. Sometimes all a person needs is to come across those who will inspire him or her to change for themselves. Is it fair that we give up on people because of what they've done in the past? Is it fair that we define people by their past rather than their progress toward their future? Be the person to inspire others to change if you can, and if you can't, then don't destroy them by confining them to what they've done before. Don't set people up for failure by showing them that they're not good enough. When you make others feel that you believe in them and that you believe that they can change for themselves, you will see what a world of a difference you can make.

After the End

Moving on may take stages,
yes.
But humans do not heal in
clear-cut steps,
no.
One moment,
you may feel completely healed,
and the next moment,
the scent of a breeze
that reminds you of them
breathes the pain so freshly
back into your flesh
and rips your heart
into pieces
once again.
You forgive them one day,
and the next day your
self-worth
screams
into every vein of yours,
paralyzing you,
begging you
to be angry with them.

Some spend a lifetime
healing,
and some spend a lifetime
wanting to heal.

Self-forgiveness

You told me that you were broken
and that you wanted to heal.
I did not know that your soul was glass.
I did not know that your heart was dark.
You aimed the broken pieces of your soul at my heart like arrows.
I broke my soul trying to mend yours.
My fingertips bled as I
weaved your soul back together.
And my eyes dried up from the tears of my pain.
I always believed that pain cleanses your soul as rain cleanses the
earth.
So I let my heart storm through my eyes.
And once your soul came back together,
you told me that
I was broken.
You told me that you were not a doctor
and that your words were just words.
You told me to move out of your way,
because who would want a wounded soul like mine?
And now I turn to my heart.
I turn to myself to say:
My dear heart,
forgive me.
Forgive me for breaking you as I healed others.
Forgive me for making you beat to the happiness of others.
Forgive me
for not listening to you.
I promise you from today—
I promise you from this moment—
to put you first.
And put me first.

Now I realize
the power of
forgiving myself.

My Door Is Now Closed

If it's my forgiveness that you want,
take it.

It is not for you
but for me.

Take it and walk away,
but don't you wait for more.

The doors you closed have been welded shut.
And the keys have been thrown into the heart of the sky.

The Day I Decided to Forgive You

Today,
I decided to forgive you.
Not because you apologized
or because you acknowledged
the pain that you caused me
but because my soul
deserves
peace.

I will not deny my soul
its rights.

Forgive Them

Forgive them,
not because they asked for your
forgiveness
or because they deserve it
or because the pain they caused you
is not worth it
but because you cannot truly
move on
without forgiving.
It shows your level of maturity and
your ability to
understand that life is not always fair
and that someone's behavior
speaks of them,
not you.
Your forgiveness speaks of you,
not them.

*I thought that I needed your apology to
move on.
I really needed to forgive myself
first.*

My Dear Self

I apologize.
For not putting you first.
For putting them first.
For making your worth dependent on how
they
saw
you.
For making their words more important than
yours.
For not allowing myself to forgive you or
to forgive me.

Forgive me.

For believing them when they said that
something was wrong with you.
Forgive me for not believing in
you.
Forgive me for loving them more than
loving you.
Forgive me for
not loving you.

My heart cries every time I read this.

Every day, tell yourself this:

Keep your heart kind
no matter how dark the world gets.
You own only yourself.
You can only control your actions.
Keep your heart beautiful.
The world needs that.

I say it to myself
too.

You think that time will change them. It won't. You think that they'll realize their mistakes with time and run to you for forgiveness. They won't. They will not. They. Will. Not. Let it sink in. Narcissists always believe that they are right. Once you become nothing to them, you are absolutely nothing. And after you expose their true colors, they start seeing you as the devil and run the other direction when you should be the one running away, further making you feel like you're not worthy of their presence. It will bother you that they can be so heartless when they are the ones at fault. But remember: At least you have a heart. At least you can feel. Be grateful for that.

Fall asleep with nothing
but love and forgiveness
in your heart.
What's meant for you
will be there for you
tomorrow or the day after.

Trust your journey.
Rest your soul.

I know that forgiveness is best,
but I hope that you never ask
for mine,
because
I don't believe
I am ready to forgive you.
I will feel like I have to
because
that is who I am.
My heart aches if I don't forgive
when I am asked,
and you've gotten used to asking.
You make mistakes
because
you know that I will forgive them.

If I am not worth your apology,
you are not worth me carrying
the pain that you caused me.
So I will forgive you, not for you
but for me.
I deserve to let go.
I deserve to be free of your pain.
And if you
can't admit your own mistakes,
I will not allow the ashes that your pain
turned me into
to hold me hostage.

Don't forgive them because
you *have* to
but because you *want* to.
And don't forgive them when
you *have* to
but when *you are ready.*

CHAPTER 2
LETTING GO

Let Go

We often attach letting go to negativity because we take it as giving up, and giving up is a sign of weakness. That's not always true. Sometimes letting go can be as positive as holding on, and sometimes holding on can be as negative as letting go. Letting go of what makes you miserable is the right decision to make because while one opportunity that you are holding on to makes you cry your heart out, another opportunity is patiently waiting for you. It is patiently waiting for you to let go of what you have and hold on to this new opportunity. When you let go of what you have, do it the right way. Don't let go feeling weak. Don't let go feeling like you've done anything but your absolute best. Don't let go feeling like you were not worth the opportunity. It was not meant to be worth your pain, although it may have been painful. Think deeply into the purpose that made you take that opportunity, and if you've achieved that purpose, then take pride in it. Give yourself credit, and don't ever let anybody put you down. Let go feeling like the biggest winner, and let loss go home with the opportunity that never appreciated you. Reflect. Learn. Move on. Hold on to the next exciting thing that the world opens up for you, and put your best forward, for your best will never let the inner you down. Ever.

Follow Your Soul

No one knows what you need to do more than you do. Cry when you need to. It's relieving. Laugh when you need to. It's healing. Sit alone when you need to. It's necessary. Surround yourself with strangers when you need to. It's eye-opening. Living by your needs is not easy. No one said it was. But a fact that you should always remember is this: You are more worthy of being taken care of than anyone around you. And I don't mean the superficial kind of care. I mean the care that your soul needs. Everyone around you is struggling somehow. Everyone around you is trying to reach a goal, a destination, or a dream. Just as you might not expose your worries to the world, no one else has to. Remember that you are a work in progress. You are not perfect. You are not expected to be. Do not allow the fear of falling to stop you from jumping. Do not allow the fear of responsibility to stop you from committing. Do not allow the fear of exposure to stop you from shining.

A Serene State of Mind

If you're not at peace with your thoughts, don't expect anyone to express theirs to you. If you're not at peace with your feelings, don't expect anyone to be honest with you about theirs. If you can't be at peace with the closest people to you, don't expect new people to enter your life. If you're not at peace with your past, don't expect a hopeful future to come easily. Peace starts from within. It reflects on your outside, whether you are aware of it or not. It is the beauty of your soul that reflects the purity from within you. Be at peace with yourself so that you may be content and happy with being who you are, or else you will be living in conflict with no one other than yourself, and you will become in need of help from someone who is not you. Don't depend on anyone to answer your questions. Don't depend on anyone to give you clarity. Find the answers yourself. Find clarity yourself. You have a brain to guide you and a heart to motivate you.

Take It or Leave It

Be the one to always give and not expect anything in return. Give, not to avoid being hurt but to feel content with what you can do yourself, to be independent, to be happy without needing anyone to give you happiness. Be like a breeze of change that inspires others to see their abilities without needing you to stay. Make people think. Make them wonder, and let them know that what you give is only based on what they are willing to take. Don't attribute your success based on whether you make a difference with everyone you meet but on the kind of difference you are willing to make. Accept that you have no ownership over people even if you do give them more than you receive. The effort that you put into inspiring others to value their own selves, and to see the best in themselves, gives them two choices: either to take it or leave it. Whatever they choose is not a sign of your success or failure unless you believe that to be the case.

Lesson Learned

Sometimes we get so stuck on fixing things that we forget that it could be more worth it to throw them out. And sometimes it's not the things that are broken but the way we think of them, because of the past they remind us of or the fact that we think of them in the first place. That's why it's good to have people in your life who will tell you when you're wrong or when you need to stop thinking. Not people who will tell you what you want to hear but people who will tell you what you need to hear so that you may truly be a better person and perceive reality the way it is, not the way you think it is.

Choose to Let Go

Letting go does not mean
that you are
giving up
or that you are
weak.
It could just mean that
you are no longer
allowing what hurts you
to control you.

Even if they
are the ones who want
you
to let go of them,
tell yourself that you are
letting them go because
you
want to.
You are not obeying
them.
You are liberating
your soul.

Make the Choice to Let Go

Just like you made the choice to
hold on,
you can make the choice to
let go.
And if it's hard, then
it must mean that you held on too tightly.
Be proud of your sincerity with your
feelings,
but realize that if holding on
is hurting you, then
you
must
let
go.

My Heart Tells Me Every Night

Let go of the hurt.
Let go of the pain.
Stay pure,
as you've always been.
Forgive them.
Forgive yourself.
Release them.
Release yourself.
Tomorrow is a new day.
Fall asleep with nothing
in your heart but
love.

My Saddest Goodbye

You will always be
my saddest goodbye.
And the most heartbreaking
story I will ever tell.
You will always be
the hardest lesson I had
to learn
when I did not want to
and
the reason I learned
to never
put someone before me.
You will always be
the best thing that
never
happened to me.
Thank you for walking away.
If you had not let go of me,
I would not have
what I have
today.

I would not be
who I am
today.

Choose Happiness

Sadly ever after
happens too,
when we find it so hard to
let go of what we invested
so
much
time
in.

I would rather let go of years
of investing in the wrong person
and be in pain
than continue to choose
sadness.

An Endless Perhaps

When I was struggling with letting you
go,
I wish someone had told me:

I know that you're struggling,
and I know that it's hard.
Believe me when I tell you that
I know why you put up that guard.
Perhaps they ignore you.
Perhaps they don't care.

Perhaps they won't tell you
how it is that they feel.

Perhaps they abandoned you
or little by little are letting go of you.

Perhaps you even have no one
to relate this poem to.
I can't tell you that it will get better,
because that's probably what they all say.
What I can tell you is that I understand you
and I think that you deserve better.
Don't force yourself into places where
you don't belong.
Don't force yourself to believe what
you know is not true.
I know that you're struggling,
and I know that it's hard.

I promise to stand by you
and help you take down
that guard.

Twenty Years

You chose to let me go.
My gift to you is
twenty years of
letting go of you.

When they see that you
actually moved on,
they might come back and
tell you that they are happy
that you gave them space and that
you've become in control of your
emotions.
Don't fall for that.
They only want the thrill of
having you care about them
again,
and once you do,
they will walk away.
Again.

I Will Not Wait for You to Regret Losing Me

I will not wait for you
to regret losing me.
Does the sun wait for
the earth to regret
turning?
Does the moon wait for
the night to regret ending?
The sun remains the sun,
and the moon remains the moon.
I will remain myself
with or without
your acknowledgment of
my value.

Back then,
I used to say that
I didn't want you to regret
losing me.
I wanted you to
not lose me.
I wanted you to
stay.

The Best Decision

Here is a hard truth
to accept:
You cannot make someone
love you.

Here is a harder truth
to accept:
The best decision that you
will ever make
is to stop wanting the love
of someone who
does not
love you.

In the Forest

I often close my eyes
and replay this in my heart.

You held my hand so tightly
and took my breath away
as you softly sealed my lips with your finger.
"Slow down. Rest your soul," you said.
And with your other hand,
you shed darkness over my eyes.
With that, you stole the beats of my heart.
"I'm scared," I said.
"I know the way," you said.
We walked and walked.
We talked and talked.
You put my worries to sleep.
You ignited the warmth of love in my heart.
You became part of me.
And I was you.
We were one.
We were one.
I put my heart to sleep inside yours.
And when I opened my eyes to the sun in yours,
I saw only the sun.
Not you.
You left and stripped the heart out of me.
I am still in the forest,
lost without a map,
waiting for you to come back
and show me the way.
You said you knew the way,
remember?

I still cry every time I read this.
I still don't understand
why you left
and never came back.

Let Them Go

Sometimes,
the best thing you can do
for someone you love
is let them go.
Set them free.
Wish them happiness and
set them free.

Set yourself free.

Let Go

They say that, at some point, you just learn to let go. I must disagree. If it just takes one moment to let go, then you never really held on tightly enough. To a dream. To a goal. To a place. To a person. To anything. I believe that you let go little by little. You let go a little, then hold back on, but with a little less force until you fully release yourself. And the tighter you hold on, the more force you let go with. The deeper you dive, the higher you'll fly. The closer you get, the further you'll pull away. The weaker you feel, the stronger you'll become. So do not be ashamed of your weaknesses. We all have them. You must learn to be kind to yourself. You must learn to understand yourself. You must believe in yourself. Never think that you are a bad person. Differentiate between your self-worth and your actions. To say that you are bad is different than saying that you made a mistake. You can't fix yourself, but you can fix a mistake. And remember, not one person on this earth is perfect. We all make mistakes. We all fall. We all have flaws. We just need to look within ourselves and treat ourselves as humans who are worthy of respect and hope. Do not give up on yourself. Get back up. Be brave. Be happy.

There Is No Right Way to Heal

I always know how to start but
never know how to end.
I am learning to let go of
what I cannot control.
I am learning to be okay with
stories that end
in the middle.
I am learning that there is no
right way
to end.

Stories that mean
something
to us
never end when or how
we want them to.
But for new stories to begin,
old ones must end.

When we must let go of someone we love, we often wonder: *Why can't they love me? Is something wrong with me? Am I not good enough?* We start to equate our self-worth with how willing they are to love us, when the truth could be that it simply wasn't meant to be. The person who is meant for you, the person who is meant to give you the kind of love that you need, and, more importantly, the kind of love that you deserve, could be somewhere out there just waiting for you to notice them. Stop fixating on someone who gave you a feeling for a short period of time. You don't deserve to spend the rest of your life convincing someone of why they should love you.

I do not want anyone to tell me
I am overthinking this.
I just want someone to
love me through this.

If your heart hurts a little after letting go of someone or something, that's okay. It just means that your feelings were genuine. No one likes endings. And no one likes pain. But sometimes we have to put things that were once good to an end after they turn toxic to our well-being. Not every new beginning is meant to last forever. And not every person who walks into your life is meant to stay.

I am free,
not because
you let me go.
I am free because
I let you go.
And set myself free.

CHAPTER 3
SADNESS

Delusion

I wonder what's worse, disappointment in reality or feeling indifferent about whether reality changes or stays the same. Life never turns its back on you. You turn your back on yourself when you allow every closed door to stop you from moving on to the next one. Sometimes we choose to stand at a closed door and hope that it will somehow open, although that may defy logic and although we may know deep down that no goodness will come from it. We wait. We choose to wait. We choose to have hope, and we're always scared that the door will open the second we walk away. We claim ownership over what we do not have and fear losing it, although it really never was ours. We read too much between the lines of hope that we weave in our own mind's imagination, only to figure out at the end that we have woven a web of fragile hopes upon fragile hopes. And just as with a spider's web, once one thread is broken, the whole web falls apart.

Hollow Hopes

We often build hopes and dreams on assumptions created by our own minds. We design these hopes and dreams exactly the way we desire them to be. They become part of us, part of our own identity, because we authentically created them. An assumption based on something that we aspire to spurs an idea or question in the mind, and after that, every event that happens serves to either confirm or disprove that assumption. Most times, events will confirm our assumptions, not because they are clear but because they don't blatantly disprove them. Our default belief is that our assumption was real. Although this defies logic, realistically, it is a logical sequence of steps that our minds go through. Our minds draw illusions of things we love to see, and our ears hear what we would love to hear. We love the feeling of instant gratification that we get from proving our thoughts. The truth is, a million proofs of confirmation, and a million proofs of disproof, are easier than one *maybe*. Maybe yes. Maybe no. That is why we like our questions to be answered, no matter what the answer is. And, it is easier for our minds and hearts to answer with a yes than with a no because our natural instinct will push us to avoid the disappointment of a no.

An Enigmatic Feeling

Once you feel any kind of feeling once, it lives forever somewhere in your heart. It can come and go and become stronger or weaker. Whether it be a feeling of love, hatred, dislike, contentment, disappointment, gratefulness, anger, etc., one truth holds: The more you contain a feeling, the more power it has within you. This is where you have a choice: You either master that feeling or make it become your master. If you master it, your response will most likely be logical, and your actions will be planned. If you let it master you, you may end up doing spontaneous things that may seem to be heart driven. We sometimes have feelings that are so powerful that they can stop us from saying what's right or encourage us to say what's wrong. People choose to deal with their feelings in different ways: talking, art, music, writing, etc. A very common way that we think we can express our feelings is talking. What we miss, though, is that once a word is said, it dies. That's it; it's out of your control now. Whether it be good or bad, once verbalized, part of your feeling becomes placed in the hands of others. For those with a conscious mind, expressing feelings is a red line because it grants others power into our hearts. Because of that, how often do we hold back from saying what we really feel to those around us? At these points, we should reflect on the reason for holding back. Is it because of the uncertainty attached to those feelings, or is it just that we refuse to sentence our feelings to words that will not do these feelings any justice?

Contemplating Happiness

Survival is not the same as living. Smiling is not the same as laughing your heart out. Thinking is not the same as having a deep conversation. Listening is not the same as really caring. Words are nothing if they are not spoken, and feelings are doomed to be erased if they are not expressed at the right time. Sometimes we are afraid of taking that extra step that takes us from what is ordinary to what is extraordinary, that extra step toward really being happy, because happiness seems just too good to be true. It seems too far away to dream of. It seems too hard to get, too hopeless, too risky. But what's the point of realizing the extraordinary if you don't go for it? You're better off not realizing it and living a content life rather than realizing it and feeling hopeless about it. There is nothing wrong with what's ordinary, but if extraordinary chances come your way, let the happiness that your heart desires extend out and reach for them.

When Sadness Is the Only Home That Welcomes You

I often come back to
the memories of you
and the pain of you,
not because I want to
be in pain,
not because I don't want to
move on,
but because they are a
home
that welcomes me
more than my
reality
does.

When you find comfort in
sadness,
it means that you need to
feel it
and walk it
gently
out of your
soul.

When Sadness Builds a Home Inside of You

Some kinds of sadness
don't leave us,
not because we want
to be sad
but because we want
to keep reminding
our souls
of how brave they were
to overcome such
pain.

I hope that
you have the courage
to allow peace
into your soul,
because you are peace,
and peace is you.
You deserve peace,
and peace deserves
you.

I See Sadness in Your Eyes

I see sadness in your eyes,
and I don't understand it.

I don't understand why it's there,
and I don't understand why I see it.

Tell me, where did you get the strength
to build a home for sadness in
the sea of your eyes?

Did you use bricks of tears to build its walls?
Did you make a garden around it with every love
that you loved
that broke you?

Tell me, did you protect it with every hollow hope
you had?

Open the door
and let it leave.

Allow happiness to colonize this home.

*I wish someone told me this
when sadness drowned my heartbeats.
So I say it to
you.*

Leave Me to My Sadness

Leave me to my sadness if
you
do not
understand it.
Don't pretend to
care
if you don't.
Don't pretend to know the
way.
Because you don't.

No one does.

Lean In to Your Sadness

You know the kind of sadness that
makes you want to be
quiet?
That makes you want to be
alone?
Isolated?
Far, far away?
That makes you want to reevaluate
everything in life?
That's not sadness.
It's an awakening within you.
Don't ignore it.
Let it overtake you so you,
yes you,
may overtake it.

The Day We Decided It's Best to Part Ways

My tears silently streamed
down my face.
You raised your hand
to wipe my tears but
put it back down when
you realized that could
hurt us both.
You told me:
"I don't want you to be sad."
I looked at you when
I did not want to, and
I told you:
"There will always be
sadness
when it comes to you
because
you will always be the one
I want to be with,
but
fate will never
destine that for us."

Rain

I am tired of looking
out the same window,
remembering the moments
I was happy when
I looked out,
because
now all I feel is
sadness over
that happiness
no longer being there.

Rainy days
and rainy windows
imprint moments on
our hearts.

Other Places

What will you say when they ask you,
"Why did you let her go?"
If it was her sadness,
that is what made her real.
If it was her sensitivity,
that is what made her considerate.
If it was her unconditional love for you,
that is what made her loyal to you.
But it's true, you know,
that we walk away from what is real
because we're too afraid
of staying in one place.
She built a home for you,
but you still had other places to see.

If It Hurts Your Soul, Let Go of It

You left my soul
through my
tears.
Extracting you from
inside of me
took the sadness
out of me.

It Will Be Painful

Believe me when
I tell you that
the sadness in your soul
will leave.
And trust me when
I tell you that
you have the power
to decide when
you want it to leave.
It will be painful.
It will be a mountain.
It will be an uphill battle.
But once you finally
cleanse it out,
happiness will trickle in
like raindrops
quenching the thirst of your
soul.

Don't move the mountain.
Climb it.

There is a sadness attached
to some endings that
no beginning
can ever erase.

Scarred Eyes

Sometimes,
a stranger can
look into your eyes
once
and not only see
but fully understand
your sadness.
No words.
No conversations.
You just both know.
You just both get it.
And you wonder how it took
moments for a stranger
to see what those around you,
for years,
did not see.

Our eyes reflect the scars
carved into our souls.

Dusty Butterflies

You promised not to walk away,
so I built a home for you
inside my heart.
Your voice,
your promises, and
your laugh
filled it with life
and love.
And now all I hear when I enter is
the echo of
your anger and
your deafening silence
that I never deserved.
So I fall to my knees and
I crumble in the corner where
I once dreamt you'd hold me.
And I choke on the dust of the
butterflies
that fell from my stomach for you
and the tears that
hailed
from my eyes for you.

An end
does not have to be
the end.

Give your heart time to heal.
The poison of pain took time to enter.
It will take time to leave.

Just as you need to
own your pain,
you need to
own your healing.

CHAPTER 4

OVERCOMING PAIN

Broken Wings

Don't break a bird's wings and then tell it to fly. Don't break a heart and then tell it to love. Don't break a soul and then tell it to be happy. Don't see the worst in a person and expect them to see the best in you. Don't judge people and expect them to stand by your side. Don't play with fire and expect to stay perfectly safe. Life is about giving and taking. You cannot expect to give bad and receive good. You cannot expect to give good and receive bad. Does it happen? Yes, but don't make that an excuse for you to keep doing what you know is wrong. Don't blame life for what you do.

Questions Unanswered

The questions that you have may be too long, too complicated, or just confusing. A mighty ship lost in the ocean may be stuck in troubled waters, calm on some days and raging on others. So are we in times of hardships and in times of uncertainty. We feel trapped when no trap can contain the amount of agony that we have. We feel our hearts caged when no cage can contain the amount of heartache that we have. Happiness and sadness swing us between the shores of anger and forgiveness. Our hearts may ache for an answer, but the truth is, the lack of an answer is sometimes better than the presence of a lie.

Feel Me

I can point you toward the sky, but I can't make you reach for the stars. I can show you the moon, but I can't make you feel its beauty or appreciate its light. I can show you the pathways that you can take, but I can't make you walk down them. I can extend my hand to help you, but I can't make you hold it. I can tell you the truth, but I can't make you believe it. I can tell you how I feel, but I can't make you care.

A Dialogue with Myself

So you go on with your daily life, interacting with people for the most part. Once the night settles its darkness upon you with that imaginary breeze tickling your eyelids softly, causing them to helplessly close, all you have is a confrontation with yourself. Are you who you want to be? Are you really who you seem to be? There's no pretending here. It is you having a heart-to-heart with yourself. One thing that we often miss is that, when fooling others, we are only fooling ourselves. We have habits that we would rather live with than get rid of. We have unspoken words that we would rather keep hidden and rest than speak loudly and show a different side of ourselves. If we don't work on changing that hidden side of ourselves, it will surface one day, regardless of how hard we try to hide it. All I'm saying is, before trying to be honest with others, be honest with yourself. Don't be afraid to take risks and say what's in your heart. Don't risk losing what matters because of the fear of disappointment in yourself or in others.

The Journey

Sometimes it's more important to figure out where you are than to decide where you're going. If you don't know where you are, how do you expect to know your destination? We often rush to our next goal, forgetting what we are leaving behind, forgetting those we are leaving behind. We forget that happiness is a journey, not a destination. We forget that tomorrow would not exist without today, and that today would not be what it is without who we are and what we have.

The Heart's Aches

Could it be that you have fallen in love with the unknown? Ask me, as I have fallen way too deep. Could it be that you miss a place you've never been? Or that your fate sends a calming feeling to your heart telling it that happiness is coming its way? Could it be that your heart smiles before your eyes do? Or that you shine just like a star in someone's sky? In a different world, in a different place, oceans away yet skies too close, a heart of gold may be waiting for the perfect moment to flutter your heart with the happiness of your dreams. One day, you will understand what you haven't heard yet and hear what hasn't been said yet. One day, you will hear silence and read what hasn't been written yet.

I Do Not Want You to Stay

One day,
you will tell me that
you wish you had never left.
And I will tell you that
I wish you had never come back,
that I wish that you had not walked away.
But you did walk away.
You will tell me that you missed
the look of love in my eyes.
And I will ask you if you missed
the tears that my eyes cried
the day that you walked away.
You will tell me that you wish
I would give you another chance.
And I will tell you that I wished
you never walked away
when you walked away.
But you still walked away.
You will tell me that you were not
yourself when you walked away.
And I will tell you that I was not
myself when I thought that
you were the one.
So do me a favor and walk away,
this time because I do not
want you to stay.

*Now I know that it's important
to realize the power I have
over your presence in my life.
Even though you chose to walk away,
it doesn't mean that I was abandoned.
I could choose to walk the other way too.*

I Do Not Want Your Love

I do not hate you,
but I hate that I allowed
your hate
to make me
hate me.

Even if you came begging for me,
I do not want your love
because
I finally learned
that I don't need you
to love
me.

Do You Know?

Do you know what it feels like to be put on a racetrack
and told to run
and run and run
with no end in sight?

Do you know what it feels like to continue on a road
that you know has no destination,
just because you are afraid of not having any other road
if you left the one that you're on?

Do you know what it feels like to be forced to jump
off a cliff,
knowing that you have no wings
to lift you?

Do you know what it feels like to shout
and scream
and yell
your heart out,
knowing that everyone is listening
but pretending not to hear?
I do.

Do you know what it feels like to believe
that you are a mistake
and that feeling pain
means that you have no control of your feelings?

Do you know what it feels like to be given the shovel
to dig deeper and deeper
only to find out when it's too late
that it's for yourself
and that there's no one waiting
to lift you out of the hole?
Do you know what it feels like to fight a battle
with no possible pain inflicted upon anyone
but yourself?

Do you know what it feels like to be wounded
and told that you caused the
wound to yourself by choosing to be where
the harm landed?

Do you know what choking on
injustice
feels like?

Do you know what it feels like to know that silence
is your best choice
when your words can no longer
be held inside of you as a
hostage?

I hope you never know that feeling,
because that is how you made me feel.
And I would never wish this kind of
pain
upon anyone.

Darling.

There are those who will light up your sky
and those whose skies you will light up.

There are those who will love you for who you are
and those whom you will crave being yourself around.

There are those who will dive into your ocean
and those whose depths you will want to drown in.

There are those who will make your heart flutter with happiness
and those whose hearts will flutter at your sight.

There are those whom you will love
and those who will love you.

And if the ones you love
love you back,
darling, you will forever see joy.

But if they feel the same way you feel about them toward someone else,
darling, that will be a disaster.

You may be a disaster for a day,
a month,
or a year.

Just don't be a disaster forever.

Find the harbor of safety.
And find the one who feels about you
the same way you feel about them.

I wrote this to myself and
to every broken soul
out there.

The Pain of Your Silence

The moments that you choose to be
silent
when someone's soul is
screaming at you,
begging you to say,
"My heart is with you,"
those moments leave
scars on our souls
that no amount of excuses can
erase.
If you love someone,
you love them.
You don't allow your pride to
stop you from expressing your love
to them.
If you expect them to understand
your love through silence,
don't be surprised when their soul
slips out of your hands in silence.

It's painful,
you know,
to not know what you mean anymore
to the one whose love was louder than
thunder
at first.

For Every Time You Ignored Me:

You make me
wait for you to
decide
that talking to me
is what you need.
You make me feel like
what I have to say is not important.
You silence me
through your silence.
You cage my heart
through your selfishness,
and when I ask you why
you're so quiet,
you tell me that
I am being selfish.

Forgive me, your highness,
for taking away from your time.
If you truly cared,
you would apologize for ignoring me,
rather than
bury me
deeper into the ground.

Let the Pain Hurt

Why do you love feeling
when you fall in love but
hate it when you're in
pain?
How do you expect pain to leave you if
you
do not
feel it
so it can leave
you?

Let it hurt you.
Let it drain you.
Let it destroy you.

For only after your destruction will you
rebuild an extraordinary masterpiece of
your soul and say:
"I own all that I am."

So go ahead. Crumble.

What Trauma Feels Like

I am still
bleeding from my
first wound.

Gaslighting of the Soul

They do everything to
dim
your light,
and then they ask you why
you're not shining.

What Truly Haunts Me

It is our
story
that haunts me,
not wanting you back
into my life.

It is not you that I
cannot get over.

It is the pain and
the wounds that keep
bleeding every time I think of you
or hear your name.
It is the scars that I have to hide
everywhere I go
that I cannot get over.

When I think of you,
I don't see your face anymore.
I see a shadow.
I see pain.
Yes, I
see
pain.

If they take advantage of your vulnerability, they should be ashamed, not you. Vulnerability takes courage. Taking advantage takes cowardice. And though the world may be filled with people ready to take advantage of your purity, don't let them taint your heart. The world might bring you down for being your kind self, but don't let that change you. The world might push you to believe that there is no place for good people, but don't let that stop you from believing in goodness. And if you struggle with the darkness out there, the world might convince you that you're too sensitive. But don't let that stop you from feeling. If feeling the pain of unfairness makes you sensitive, then may we all be sensitive. What I'm trying to say is, if you make the choice to be a good person regardless of how the world treats you in return, be proud of that. It makes you a hero. A gem. A true human.

Don't let your heart become numb. No matter how much pain you're going through, the solution should never be to become numb. The solution is to accept that any harm that was aimed at you is not your fault. And the pain that others choose to inflict on you is not because of who you are but because of who they are. If you become numb just to avoid the pain, then you won't be able to feel happiness either. Feel the pain, and resist the temptation to avoid it. If you can do that, you're a hero.

When home doesn't feel like home:
I drive around in circles
hoping to get to a destination—
one where I would be happy.
The right place.
The right time.
But it seems so impossible.

Where I leave from and
where I arrive
feel the same.

I just want to breathe,
and I am gasping for air,
but my lungs feel too small.
I guess that is what happens when
your lungs enter
survival mode—
they breathe only as much
as they need
to stay alive.

This air that wants to
enter you
and this love that wants to enter you
have no room to stay inside of you.
That's why it's so hard
for you to accept
new love.
It's too much to handle.

I feel that I am on the verge
of disappearing,
of surrendering into nothingness,
of accepting that I am worth
absolutely nothing
and that I deserve what happened to me.
And everything that it did to me.
I have no power.
Where do I get it from?

No one has the right to judge the pain inside of your heart. They are not the ones who sit by your bedside when you cry yourself to sleep at night. They are not the ones who carry the mountains on your shoulders as you get through the day. They are not the ones who are wondering where your happiness went. They are not the ones aching to smile again. No one should ever judge a pain they've never felt. Those who love you don't judge you. They listen to you. They understand you. And they love the pain out of you. They don't try to beat the pain out of you by denying you the right to feel it. So don't feel ashamed that you're in pain just because someone makes you feel that you have no right to feel it.

The past is behind you
for a reason.
Don't go back to it
hoping that it will change.
No one can change history.
It already happened.
No one can make a day that ended
start again.
If you try to change the past,
it will only break you again.

You are bigger than
what's pulling you down.
Shake the ashes
off your wings and
rise.
Fly.
Soar.

When you are tempted
to wish them pain,
remember how it felt
when they hurt you.

Never wish them pain.
That's not who you are.
If they caused you pain,
they must have pain inside.
Wish them healing.
That's what they need.

It's okay for you
to be angry about
what happened to you.
Just don't let your anger
make you like the one
who broke you.
Stay true to yourself.

CHAPTER 5

REBUILDING YOURSELF AFTER ABUSE

Goodness Gone Wrong?

When someone you've done so many good things for makes you feel unappreciated, do you, even for a moment, wish that you could take it all back? Do you regret doing good things for the wrong people? Personally, I don't agree with that. At the end of the day, everything you do belongs to you. All of your actions belong to you, whether good or bad, for yourself or for others, intentional or unintentional. Instead of regretting doing something good for the wrong person, it is better to regret taking that time away from those who do good things for you. Don't ever regret a good deed. Ever. As much as it hurts to see that someone does not appreciate your work, your work is really not for them. Your work builds you and your personality. This is where you need to think of your purpose behind anything you do. If your purpose is to please others and look good in their eyes, then you are bound to be disappointed because your pleasure is in their hands, not yours. If your purpose is to truly and sincerely be a good person who spreads a positive and mature attitude that rises above individual needs, then you will be disappointed less often and in a different way. You will be disappointed that someone, regardless of who this person is, could be so blind and ungrateful for something good. You will be disappointed for them, not in them. Think of your purposes and work on yourself. Once we realize that we need to change the way we view the world before we try to change others, our purposes will be geared in the right direction.

Heal

Don't point out people's mistakes unless you're willing to tell them how to fix them. Criticism can break the strongest of souls, and advice can build the weakest of spirits. Your words can be healing, or they can be sickening. Let them heal. Let them inspire. Let them be the crying shoulder that your shoulder cannot be.

Take Responsibility

Don't rely on others to make your life better. You may seem like a puzzle piece that fits nicely into their plans at one point, but what happens if they change their minds? So be it. You have a mind to lead you by logic and a heart to lead you by reason. You choose your fate by taking responsibility and by taking the lead in your life. Don't make yourself part of others' plans. Make your own plan and be part of it.

The Vicious Cycle of Rudeness

An important lesson that I've had to learn over the years is that, if I respond to people's rudeness to me by mistreating those who care for me, then I have become like those who were rude to me in the first place. What is the point of putting the people who are good to you down because of others putting you down? Isn't it a vicious cycle of people being victims of rudeness? Turn that negative energy that you receive from people into a positive attitude by appreciating the goodness around you. It will bounce back to you and keep you going. A smile is a beautiful human expression, so when you receive it from someone, don't return it with a frown but let your natural humane instinct kick in and smile back.

Broken Promises

If they break the promises that they once made, it does not mean that you were not worth making these promises come true. It means that they are no longer willing to put in the effort to live up to their words. You did your part by believing their words. And that's what good people do. Even if there is a chance the other person is lying, we believe them. Not because we are naive. But because we believe *in* them. We believe in their ability to fulfill the words they have said. We know that it's much easier to give up on someone than it is to make a difference in their lives by being someone who believed in them.

Your Opinion of Me

Sometimes it hurts more to stay away from what hurts you than to keep allowing it to hurt you. That's why you make excuses when they don't exist. That's why you create hope that, ironically, makes you hopeless. That's why you put locks on doors before you try to open them. Life is simple. Love is everywhere. You just have to change where you're looking. You have to change what you're seeing. See the best in yourself before you see it in others because, if you can't see the best in yourself, you will come to believe the worst that people believe of you. You will fool yourself into believing that their opinion of you is essential to your happiness. Be honest with yourself for a moment. Those who see the impact that they have on your life and choose to use it in a manipulative way do not belong in your life. A true leader will tell you to stop following him if he notices that you're following. A manipulative person will be happy to see your willingness to do whatever is asked of you. I'm not saying that you need to remove these people from your life. I'm just telling you to stop associating your happiness with theirs if they don't consider you a part of it. Stop equating your worth with their opinion of you.

The Way Home

Even though your eyes
speak of the
broken promises that
someone once made,
someone's eyes
somewhere
will speak of
the love that they have for your
brokenness.

All of the places that let
you
go
are leading you to
your
home.

Homes Stay

You were my home
for so long.
Now I realize that humans
cannot
be homes.
If homes can leave,
then they are not
homes.
Homes stay,
but you walked
away.

Your Wanting of Me

Take your memories with all your pain.
Take it all.
I want to be free.
It was not your love that you chained me with
but your wanting of me.
I used to think that happiness was not possible
before I saw you regretting
walking away from me.

But now I know that if a man like you
had the heart to walk away from a woman like me,
what is the use of having you regret
leaving me?

I have been dwelling in a dark place,
thinking that if
you
left me,
then something must be wrong
with me.

Streets

If you knew how many streets I avoid
to avoid you
and memories of you,
you would leave your streets
and your cities.
If the streets I avoided to avoid you
and memories of you
knew,
they would change their names
so you
could find other streets
to put your footsteps on.

If only you knew.

The day that uncertainty finally
ended my patience with you

I said:

"I am so tired of
not knowing
what I am to you.
So I decided to
walk away and
send my love to you
through thoughts
and prayers."

You said:

"Take a step back.
You're overthinking again.
Take a deep breath."

I look back, and I wish
I had told you,
"I am not
your patient."

The Verdict

We sat in the office of the judge,
the one who was meant to help us
end in peace.

I told you that
if you told me that
you truly cared about me
and that you decided to walk away
for reasons other than
who I am,
I would forgive you.
You looked down at your
fingertips,
looked back up,
and said:
"I did not know
that your love for me
was this deep."

That is when I knew
that you meant everything that you
ever said,
but
you did not know the depth of
your own words.

And maybe you walked away,
not because of who I am,
but because you didn't know
how big the home I built for you was.

I Am Worthy

When a new opportunity for love
comes your way,
do not judge it based on
what your last partner had that
the new one
does not have.
Do not base it on how thankful
you are that the new one
does not have the same
flaws
that the old one had that
you hated.
Base it not on how good the
new person is.
Base it on who they are.
Base it on whether their journey
fits with
yours.

In a Coffee Shop

In a coffee shop
one day,
you will see me sitting
next to the window,
sipping on my coffee
the same way
I used to
and looking out the window
the same way
I used to.
You will wonder if I still think about you
the same way
I used to
or if I am still waiting for you to come back
the same way
I used to.

You better walk away, because
I no longer crave you in my life
the same way
I used to.

Too Fragile

I am so afraid of
giving you the pieces of
my soul that
I gave before.

They are still hurting and
perhaps too
fragile
to trust again.

To a Narcissist I Once Loved

I know that you are waiting
for me to break down and
contact you.
I know that you must be thinking
that I am miserable waiting for you
to give me attention.
But, you see,
I am not the person I once was.
You destroyed me over and over,
but I built myself back up
into someone you will
never
have the honor of
getting to know.

For Every Time I Told You That You Were Distant

I look back to the day
that I told you for the
millionth
time that I felt that
you were distant.

You could have said:
"I am with you,"
but you said:
"Please.
Stop.
Obsessing."

At that time,
I did not know that
your unwillingness to comfort me
was a sign that I needed to
walk away.

It's okay to never be okay
with what happened to you.
Just remember that
not being okay with it
does not mean that you
can't move
past it.
It might never stop never being okay,
but you will be okay.

I saw you,
and you looked like the weight
of the world was on your shoulders.
I felt guilty and
wanted to ask you
how you were doing.
But my heart reminded me:
You're the one who chose to leave.
You're the one who chose to hurt me.
You're the one who chose the end.
So I will let you deal with this pain
on your own.
If you deserved my care,
you would have loved me
when you had the chance.
So I put my heart together and
I walked away,
not because I didn't care
but because the heart that you broke
couldn't handle being broken again.

Let them judge you.
They will live with their
judgment,
and you will live
with your truth.

Strength does not mean
that you have no struggle
or that you are completely
at peace
with a hurtful past.
It means that you
don't allow the past
to make you
shrink
and fall again.

I am broken
beyond repair.

There is no going back
to the person I was before.

There is rebirth,
rebuilding,
reinventing,
and soul stitching
with gold
that needs to happen.

You can't erase
what happened to you,
but you can choose
to put it behind you,
under your feet,
and rise like
the hero you are.

I do not want anyone to tell me
to stop feeling the pain.
I do not want anyone to tell me
to let things go.

I saw you from a distance
and felt sad.
I knew you wouldn't come to me
like you used to.
But you did come to me
like you used to
and lay by my side
like you used to.
You ran your fingers
across my face
and the creases of my hands
like you used to.
You were gentle with me
and took a few moments
to look deeply into my eyes
like you used to.
My soul flooded with happiness,
but soon I woke up
from my dream
because you no longer love me
like you used to.

You seek pain as if
it's going to save you.
You dip into sadness
as if it's going to bring you joy.
You expect that loving
the night will make
your days better,
and that loving the rain
will make the sun shine brighter.
You expect that diving
into the ocean
will get you to the shore of sanity
faster.

You're not the only one
who's not happy.
Trust me.
All you see is what you want
but don't have.

People like you are hiding
behind smiles,
pretending to be happy
while they're wondering
why they don't have what
others have,
just like you are.

From the ashes,
I rose
and I stitched the pieces
of my soul
back together
with gold.

When they make the mistake
and you have to apologize,
know that there is a problem
and walk away.

It's easier for them to believe
that something is wrong with you
than it is for them to believe
that something wrong happened to you.

Your biggest loss was me.
My biggest loss was me.

CHAPTER 6

SELF-CONFIDENCE

Transparent Heart

Sometimes people make obvious what's in their hearts, not necessarily through words but indirectly through their actions. Do we make what's in our hearts as obvious in return? Sometimes we try so hard to hide our thoughts and feelings because we are scared of the unknown. We are scared that, once our thoughts and feelings are exposed, they will not be taken care of by others the way we took care of them for so long. We are scared of letting go of what is in our control and putting it in someone else's hands. We take a step ahead, and because of that fear, we take ten steps backward, not realizing that we are causing that same fear for others. We are scared of being misunderstood. And because of this, we linger in a state of uncertainty, not knowing what to do because all we know is what we see and not what we hear. Although feelings are much stronger than words, it somehow brings ease to our hearts and minds to hear what we would like to hear before we can let go of that fear. We forget that, sometimes, simply saying what needs to be said can make any trace of uncertainty in others turn into a confidence that cannot be defeated.

Work Hard

Thirty years from now, what do you want to look back and tell yourself? If you keep in mind the purpose you have in your life, every hard day becomes worth it. So, if you're working hard, work harder. Don't give up. Don't ever stop. Building yourself, though it is exhausting, is more rewarding than the regret of not doing so, especially when you realize that you're not as strong as you once were or as capable as you once were.

Baby Steps

Today, promise yourself to be the best that you know you can be at whatever you do. Celebrate the little steps and little successes that you have, no matter how small you think they are. No step toward your dreams is too small. Those little steps are like the beginning of the storm of good things that will hit you; starting with the little steps, the raindrops fall slowly and softly. Don't expect to be an expert at whatever you do from day one. Be realistic. Be up for the journey. Prepare yourself for the victory by staying humble about your achievements.

Be a Treasure

Treasures are sought because they are unique. They are different. They are timeless, despite the time that passes after they come to existence. They are not easily found because, to get to them, one must work hard. One must dig deep. One must appreciate the value at hand. You are deep. You are valuable. So let others dig you up.

Know Yourself

Have that wise instinct of knowing how you would react in certain situations before they happen so that you can be well prepared to react wisely. Notice patterns in your behavior and the way you react in unexpected situations so that you may prepare yourself to react better the next time. Once you master yourself, *impossible* will no longer stand in the way of your dreams.

The Rare You

People will rarely see you the way that you see yourself, but don't let it stress you out. You most likely don't see people the way they see themselves either. We selectively choose what to see in others based on our purpose of having them in our lives. We may see others the way that they like to be seen, but not the way that they really are, because what we see is only a snapshot that is bound to a certain time, to a certain angle, and to a certain state of mind that we have. Everything is relative, and nothing about you that people see is a pure truth because no one is perfect, and no characteristic in you can ever be applicable a hundred percent of the time. The only truth that holds place is that you have a certain capacity to cause a change in others based on what you can or cannot offer them. This capacity depends on your willingness to act upon it. If you believe that you can inspire others to change their ways and see themselves for who they are, and you are willing to go ahead and do it, then you are brave. You are rare. If you choose to keep that capacity within you without sharing it with those who can benefit from it, then you are no different than most people who choose to remain neutral. Which one are you?

Accept Yourself

Don't look for acceptance. Look for respect. If you get it, give it back, and if you don't, be the first to give it. If you don't get it back, keep moving forward. If you kill yourself over every person who doesn't treat you the same way that you treat them, you'll waste your time worrying about changing people who don't care about changing themselves in the first place. If you make yourself believe that you need people to accept you, then you are giving them the right to reject you. You don't need anyone to accept you. You need to accept yourself. You need to respect yourself. You can't make anyone understand you. You can't make anyone listen to you. You can't make anyone love you, trust you, or even like you. In the same way that you decide to make them important to you, give them the right to make that decision too. If they don't, it's not your responsibility to change the way they think of you. It's your responsibility to change the way you think of yourself. Before you expect people to put themselves in your shoes, put yourself in your own shoes. Worry about changing what you need to change.

A Step Forward

You know those moments when you feel stuck between moving a step forward or staying where you are, comfortable in your own place, not wanting to commit yourself to something more? Those are critical moments that we often shy away from because of the unstoppable chain of questions attached to them: What if I regret this? What if I can get something better if I wait a bit longer? What if it's not really meant for me? What if now is not the right time? etc. Taking certain steps toward your future is one of the toughest things to do because you are afraid of being stuck with something that you can't get out of. You are scared of the unknown. We wish we knew what was coming, yet we love the feeling of something new. We would rather the route of life bestow its action upon us, and accept what it gives us and deal with it, than take the lead and go out to make our own future. We would rather respond to an action than initiate an action ourselves. I do that sometimes too, but I've come to the realization that a decision not made at the right time can affect the course of a lifetime, a suitable commitment not made can change a destiny, and an opportunity for growth not taken can affect our biggest dreams. How do you determine what the right decisions, commitments, and opportunities are? This is where you take the lead. Balance your mind's logic and your heart's reason. Now make a decision, make a commitment, take an opportunity.

A Sky That No Longer Welcomes You

Asking me to understand why
you no longer love me
is like asking me to understand why
I am no longer worthy of being loved.
I am confident, and
my self-esteem is resilient, but
asking a soul to accept that
the love it once had
is no longer there
is like
telling a bird that
the sky
that it's used to flying in
no longer wants it to fly.

Every bird loves to fly
in its sky, and
every soul loves
to be loved
by the one that it loves.

Scars

Some scars are
seared
on our souls
for eternity to
witness.

.

You Really Are Not the Reason

I am tired of looking for
reasons.

I know that I am a good person.
How could
I
be the reason
for this end?

Give Your Love Back to Yourself

You love those who don't love you,
to the point of giving them your soul
if they needed it.
But you cannot love your own soul to
make sure that it is stitched together?
Isn't the love that you give them
a reflection of the love
that your soul contains?
So if they don't want that love,
why don't you give it
back
to yourself?

You become empty when
all you do is give
without giving
your own
self.

They'll Always Have Something to Judge You For

If you write about love,
they might say that you're in love.
And if you write about heartache,
they might say that you're heartbroken.
If you write about happiness,
they might wonder why you're so happy.
And if you write about sadness,
they might pretend like they didn't hear it.
If you write about loss,
they might pity you.
And if you speak the truth,
they might criticize you.
So let it be that you're in love.
Have they not been?
Let it be that you've been heartbroken.
Who is not?
Let it be that you're happy or sad.
Is it not normal?
Let it be that you've lost.
We've all lost.
But don't you ever let
what people think stop you from
expressing yourself.

Let your soul shine
through your words.

Every time he asked me
"Who do you think you are?"
the ashes that I was
burning into
would answer:
"I am no one."

When his voice
asks me now:
"Who do you think you are?"
the hero I've become
answers:
"I am Najwa Zebian.
I am a hero.
I am a survivor."

For all the times
you saw me and
pretended not to see me or
didn't want to be seen with me:

A day will come
when I will no longer
want to be seen by you or
seen around you.
It will be you
waving at me
from across the street,
and it will be me
turning in the other direction.

When a hero is rising,
many will choose
to focus on the ashes at their feet.
Keep rising.
You are about
to start soaring.

I am so proud
of the warrior
I've created
from the ashes
that were meant
to bury me.

If I lost your respect because
of what I went through,
keep your respect.
I don't want it.

CHAPTER 7

FINDING AND RAISING YOUR VOICE

Take That Step

If you can't stand up for what you believe in, prepare to be silenced. If you don't have the courage to pursue your dreams, prepare for someone else reaching them. If you don't have the strength to hold on to what really matters in your life, then prepare for it to let go of you. If you can't take the initiative to take the step forward that will give you a better future, then prepare for that future to step further away from you. Quit blaming your surroundings for the consequences that you cause for yourself. Lead your life and follow your dreams, not people.

Break Free from the Illusion of Power

The realities that we are forced to accept in life are sometimes very challenging. Most people will tell you that you need to accept the good and the bad and just be quiet, as long as you're not harmed, as long as accepting and being silent keeps you in your place or moves you forward instead of taking away from what you already have. It is sad but true. We are faced with people daily who tell us that patience is suffering in silence. We are faced with people daily who tell us that following is better than leading and that obeying orders is better than questioning those orders. They disregard the fact that questioning someone's orders or opinions is not a disrespectful act toward those individuals. My philosophy in life and my beliefs request of me to respect myself before I respect anyone else, because if respecting someone else jeopardizes my own respect, then that respect is superficial, invalid, and insincere. My beliefs force me to question everything that comes my way, regardless of where it comes from.

The Power of Words

Your words can be more healing than any kind of medicine. They can be more toxic than any kind of poison. They can ease a mind of its nagging questions. They can relieve a heart from its doubts. They can free a heart from the chains that keep it holding on and that make it fear letting go. They can spring hope into a deserted heart. They can shatter a soul barely holding on to the pieces that make it strong. They can be a shelter for the broken and a canon of motivation for those who need confidence. They can build mountains of confidence and build stairs to those dreams that hide above the clouds. They can dig holes into the darkest and deepest of scars. They can strike happiness into the souls in most need of it, and they can strike sadness into the souls of those most far away from it. So, before you speak, ask yourself if your words are true. If they are not, then you are fooling the hopeless into hope that won't last. You are breaking down walls temporarily that will be built even higher afterward. Say what the truth and genuineness in your heart need to say. Say no more.

Power

Respect the freedom that you were born with but that you've denied yourself. Break free from the power that power has over you, and believe in your own beliefs.

Stay True to Yourself

Don't worry about what people think of you or about the way they try to make you feel. If people want to see you as a good person, they will. If people want to see you as a bad person, absolutely nothing you do will stop them. Ironically, the more you try to show them your good intentions, the more reason you give them to knock you down. Keep your head up high, and be confident in what you do. Be confident in your intentions, and keep your eyes ahead instead of wasting your time on those who want to drag you back. Because you can't change people's views, you have to believe that true change for yourself comes from within you, not from anyone else.

Don't Be Shallow

What is the point of a diamond dangling on a heartless chest? Or on a deaf ear? Or on an ungenerous hand? What is the point of loving people for the way that your eyes see them, not for who they really are on the inside? Don't be the one who gets fooled by an egg dipped in gold. At the first obstacle, its beautiful covering shatters, and all that is left is nothing that will please your eyes. Use your eyes to see into people's hearts, not the way that they make their hearts appear.

Write Your Happiness

What makes your life unique? Life is full of ups and downs. It is full of good moments and bad moments, amazing times and times when you are desperate for anything good to happen. If life came with a manual, it would be full of blank pages that you would fill out yourself. There would be pages that you wish you could rip out but can't, pages that you wish you could stay on and not turn, pages that you would love to erase and rewrite. Those wishes and those feelings are what make your life unique, irreplaceable. There is no one path to happiness, no one path to uniqueness. There is no one path to success. So, instead of wasting your time looking for prescribed steps to take to make your life perfect, pave your own steps. Create your own landmarks. Walk your own path. You will not feel the greatness of your success unless you make it unique to yourself, unless you direct your strengths in the right direction and use your weaknesses to your advantage. Avoid the defined black-and-white rules set by others. Be genuine with whatever you do. Make your own colors and shine.

Pamper Your Wishes

When you make a wish, believe that it is going to happen. Put it in your heart next to passion. Next to honesty to yourself and others. Next to humility with yourself and others. Next to consideration for yourself and others. Next to believing in yourself and others. And so that the wish will be the perfect gift when it is granted to you, wrap it from the beginning with the bow of hard work and determination. Don't ever make a wish and leave it, because it will leave you too. If you can't do anything about it, then start with your heart. Believe that you are worth that wish coming true so that you can be worthy of it.

Where Am I?

Sometimes we think that we know what's going on inside of people's hearts and minds and that we are certain of our thoughts. And it makes sense because, based on our experience with them, we think that we know exactly the way they think. As hard as we try to give others the benefit of the doubt, we feel that we need to protect ourselves from their harm by expecting them to be the same as they've been before. That just makes it easier for us to perceive and understand their new actions. It's a safe feeling. The slightest inflection in their voice can have so much meaning behind it. The look they have on their faces as they are saying or asking for something can tell us whether to read into their words or whether to take them just as they are. The truth is that most of us are constantly challenged to be better than we are, and we do try to *fix* our image to be the way that we want it to be seen by those around us. Somewhere along the way of trying different things that we think will help change us, we may be misunderstood to be trying too hard, to be fake, and to be different than what we really are. Compare this to the metamorphosis of a butterfly. Halfway through, it looks nothing like what it ends up being. It is your choice to either stay halfway through or to continue your journey once you start it, to reach that destination of the person you know you can be.

Wholeheartedness

A risk that you take is only genuinely yours when you put your whole heart into it and go for it with your own convictions, not because of pressures from others. A true risk is one that you choose to take with hope that it will be a milestone for the fulfillment of your vision in life. If a risk ends positively, then you've made the right choice, and if it does not end as you hoped it would, that calls for a reflection on your part and an evaluation of the implications for new risks that you take. Either way, you learn a lesson only if you keep in mind that everything you do is a learning experience and never a waste of time. Time is only wasted when it is used for efforts that prove to be disappointing and which we regard as a waste. If we change the way we look at the disappointment, and consider it an experience that we can learn from, we add one new thing into the *shape* of our personalities. Sometimes that is just enough to make us realize the importance of spending time on what we neglected while we took that risk. When you focus on forgetting negative experiences instead of taking time to reflect on them and learn from them, you put yourself at the risk of inviting more negativity into your life, because negative thoughts will pile up, and every time you have a negative experience, you will recall all of the other times and reassure yourself that you have a bad life or bad luck. But when you learn to twist each negative event into a positive lesson and apply that lesson into your new experiences, you become more skillful at seeing the positives in life rather than the negatives. Instead of falling back on all of the *bad* things that have happened to you, you are building a good, positive bank of experiences that has, at its base, the understanding that *mistake* is too big and too negative of a word, while *experience* is bigger and more constructive to your life.

Why I Believe

Have you ever looked at the way that someone lives and thought to yourself that it just doesn't make sense? When we are born, we are acculturated into a certain set of beliefs that becomes the *right* way for us to live. It's the life that makes sense to us because that's all we know, and those beliefs become part of our identity. Anything else is new, and we avoid it because it just doesn't feel right. It makes sense to feel that way, doesn't it? You're raised into the beliefs of those who raised you because their beliefs are instilled in them and are echoed in the way they see your life progressing. Here's the catch. Are you able to defend your beliefs? Or do you just say, "That's just the way it is"? You must critically think about everything around you, because if you don't know deep inside the reasons you believe in certain things, you will lose your commitment to them at the first obstacle you come to. You have to be convinced by your beliefs, thoughts, and way of life. Think of the reasons you do what you do and the reasons you accept certain things and reject others. If there are no reasons, then work on finding them. Maybe then you can actually learn to accept that differences among humans exist and that the *right* life is relative. Take the time to evaluate your life. How can you take the lead in your own life if you've already allowed yourself to be a naïve follower in it?

Sometimes, this is all you have to say:

"You changed.
And that is painful."

Tell their voices:

No.
I am not
what you say of me.
No.
I am
what I do.
Just like you are not
what I say of you.
No.
You are
what you do.

The way that you define the beauty of me
with the pleasure that you get
out of me
says a lot more about you
than it says about me.
I am beautiful,
not because of my face,
not because of my body.
I am beautiful because of the heart
contained in this body.
I am beautiful because of the mind
controlling this body.
So if you must *grab* me by something,
let it be my heart.
It is what makes the world
a compassionate place.
If you must *grab* me by something,
let it be my mind.
It is what spreads wisdom in this world
like wildfire.
And finally, sir,
I must ask you:
If the woman in me
sees the human in you,
why can't the man in you
see the human in me?

•

If you hate me because of
what happened to me,
I don't hate you,
but
I also will not allow your hatred
of me to make me doubt myself.

I don't want to be liked
by someone whose love is
conditional on shame.

You hit me with
your pain,
and I turn it into
poetry.

To all of the lights
who chose to dim
when I was in the darkness,
thank you for teaching me
that my own light
is all I need.

If the voice inside your head
is not yours,
shut it up and
kick it out.

CHAPTER 8

STEPPING INTO YOUR OWN POWER

Listen

Stop listening to the voices around you. Focus on the voices within you. Your heart's language is the most comprehensive. Your mind's logic is the most worthy of your time. Fix yourself before you worry about fixing others. At the end of the day, no one will walk your journey for you. You have to do that. At the end of the day, no one will dream for you. You have to do that. At the end of the day, no one will lose a moment of sleep because of the sleep you lose. Learn to trust your instincts. Don't ask for advice on personal matters unless it's from family. No one has an intrinsic motive to stand up for you. If you don't want people to assume facts about you, don't assume facts about them. Teach yourself to be independent of others' opinions but respectful of them. Love solitude. Love the person that you are. Don't ever believe that you are the same as anyone else. Don't ever dare to think that being different is a crime, no matter how many people shut you out. They earned the right to be let go of. You are different, and that's a fact. You are unique, and that's a fact. Your existence is in your hands, so let it shine. Let it inspire. Let it be free.

Rest Your Heart

Your heart is precious, so take care of it. It may be able to forgive unconditionally, but don't exhaust it by surrounding yourself with those who constantly do you wrong. It may have an infinite capacity for patience, but don't exhaust it by surrounding yourself with those who don't value your time.

Make a Difference

Making a difference in the world begins with making a difference in yourself. Life may pass you by, and one day you will realize that you spent years on others and always wondered when you would have time for yourself. The truth is that it is so much easier to care for others than it is to care for yourself. Honesty hurts you, but being honest with others about themselves is a lot easier. So you invest in others. You forget that the best kind of investment is in making yourself a better person. Don't stop caring for others, but promise me this: Start caring for yourself today. Let go of whatever is holding you back. No excuses. Just start.

The Way They Treat You

Have you ever been told to treat people the way they treat you? Well, don't do that. Treat them better than they treat you. If a person's bad action makes you do the same, how can you say that you are any better? If a person discourages you from doing your own good, encourage him or her to do what's for his or her own good. Remember, you don't have to listen to them, but you also don't have to answer them back in their own tone. If a person disrespects you, react to him or her with respect. Learn from the best. Don't compare yourself by looking down. Always look up to those who struggled yet still inspired their worst enemies.

Know Your Power

Just as you can't deny that you can feel love and hate, happiness and sadness, anger and ease of mind, or tiredness and relaxation, you can't deny that you have a fate that, sometimes, you can't control. That doesn't mean that it takes control over you. You can't deny that you have words that need to be spoken. You can't deny that you have a choice. You can't deny the ability that you *can say no.* You can't deny the ability that you have the freedom to make a decision and defend it. You can't deny injustice when you see it, unfairness when you feel it, oppression when you witness it. Stop blaming the world around you for wronging you. Take responsibility for the *no*s you could have said but chose not to, the words you could have said but didn't, instead wrapping your mouth with your own hands and remaining silent against what needed to be addressed. Take responsibility for the choices you could have made but restrained yourself from taking.

It's Time to Change

The first obstacle to change is feeling the need to give those around you an excuse. You don't have to explain, but it's okay if you do. Most likely, it is those around you who have made you realize that you need to change, so why would you explain? Would you explain to someone why you're watering a withering flower? Would you explain why you're feeding a hungry person? Would you explain why you're breathing? You don't need to explain why you're protecting your soul from harm. You really don't.

The Gift of Gentleness

Not everyone you meet will give you the respect or love that you deserve. Respect them anyway. Love them anyway. No matter what you do, be kind. It is better to be kind and be hurt than to be unkind and cause pain. You were given the gift of gentleness and kindness. You were given the gift of a soft heart. So do not lose it. Do not allow your heart to harden. Just because someone caused you pain, it does not mean that everyone will. Just because someone betrayed your trust, it does not mean that others aren't trustworthy. Just because someone broke your heart, it does not mean that it will remain broken forever. It is better to love with a whole heart, to give with a whole heart, and to trust with a whole heart than to never experience the beauty of love, the reward of giving, and the comfort of trusting. And when you fall hard, you can choose to remain on the ground for as long as you want, but you can also choose to get back up. Love again. Give again. Trust again. It is the experience that grows you, not the fear of it.

I Am My Own Savior

You escaped my soul
through my tears.
My love for you was as
deep
as the ocean,
and that's how far down I dove.
I cried enough to fill the ocean
and float my soul back
to shore.

I Am Giving You Back to You

There once was a spark for you
that built a home in my eyes.
And with every step you took
further away from me,
the night sky fell into my eyes.
It turns out that not every song is worth
singing,
not every mountain is worth
climbing,
not every race is worth
running,
and not every war is worth
fighting.

I loved the parts of you that I did not
own.
And you owned the parts of me that you did not
love.

So I am taking my love back
today.
And today, I am giving
you
back to you.

Just because you choose not to
climb a mountain,
it does not mean that you have to
carry it.

Console Your Soul

It hurts me that
someone like you
hurt a kind soul like mine
and turned around to say
that something was wrong
with me.
I console myself by
reminding myself that
while I am sitting here
wondering what is wrong with
me,
you
are the one who is
broken.
You are the one who needs
fixing,
not me.
Your wings may have healed
enough to allow you to fly,
but your soul has not
healed if it has not learned
to give,
to apologize,
and to face its own truth.

If You Ever Think of Revenge

I hope one day
when the tables turn
that I am no longer
sitting at them.
I have no interest in
helping karma
take its course,
nor am I interested in treating
them
the way they treated
me.

A World of My Own

I used to think that
you accepting me into your world
would make me
the luckiest person on earth,
as if luck belongs in
places or
humans.
Today,
I am thankful that there was no place
for me
in your world.
I have created a world of my
own.
And for that,
I am lucky.

I will not thank you for this pain.
I will not thank you for this destruction.
But I thank you for this lesson:

My demolition might not be in my hands,
but my reconstruction is.

Your sensitivity is not a sign of weakness. Your sensitivity makes you beautiful. It makes you unique. You see, we live in a world where it's easier to pretend that you don't feel, and if you dare express that you feel, you become an easy target to be picked on and hurt. So, from a young age, you're taught that strength means hiding how you feel, or not expressing your feelings at all. I want you to ask yourself, if you don't feel, how can you truly love? If you don't feel, how can you empathize with the tragedies happening in the world? If you are sensitive to being disrespected, it means that you will not disrespect others because you know how it feels to be disrespected. If you are sensitive to being ignored or lied to, you will not ignore or lie to others because you know how it feels to be ignored and lied to. Promise yourself from today to be at peace with your sensitivity. Instead of trying to hide it, cherish it.

You are not
the pain that broke you.
You are who it made you become.

Look how far you've come.
You rose above
what was meant to break you.
You are soaring.
You are a hero
reborn.

Don't tell me how
or when
to heal
if you didn't live through my pain,
if your heart did not stop
and struggle
to be with mine
when I was burning
and turning to ashes.

CHAPTER 9

SELF-WORTH

An Ironic Reward for a Beautiful Heart

Beautiful hearts are hard to find, and to reward them when we do find them, we convince ourselves that they're too good for us. What a reward. Instead of holding on to them, we pull ourselves away. We push them away. We forget that the beauty of their hearts comes from their ability to love and from their willingness to liberate those whose hearts have caged themselves in the past.

The Power of Silence

Silence can hold more meaning than words. It has power to make a heartless person love and an innocent victim hate. It is much more powerful than words because it takes effort to keep. It is not only about closing your mouth. It is about taking in others' actions or words, thinking about them, formulating an answer, criticizing that answer, searching for logic from your mind and reason from your heart, and then convincing yourself that not saying the answer is better. Silence is not a sign of weakness. It is a sign of intelligence and inner power. It is a sign of faith that replying in the same manner that you were treated will only make you just as ignorant. Learn to be an observer, a deep one, who reflects not only on his or her mistakes but also on the mistakes of others.

You Are What You Give

So maybe when you care, you feel that you care too much. And when you love, you drown them in your love. Maybe when you give, you give feeling like they won't understand why you're giving so much. Something reminds you that if you don't make them work for what you give them, that you, as a person, are somehow not worthy enough of being reciprocated what you already gave. Take a step back and remind yourself of this: What you give is an indication of what you own. So if you give too much care, that care comes from somewhere within you. If you love too sincerely, that love comes from somewhere within you. What you give comes from somewhere within you. That is what defines your worth: what you give and your willingness to give it knowing that you might not get anything in return, not what they take or how they take it.

Your Inner Beauty

In an upside-down world like ours, it doesn't matter who you are. Who you make yourself seem like does, though. The higher your expectations, the harder people will work to reach them. And with your prestige, they value you more. It's true. But why do you look at materialistic people? Why do you look at those who make you feel like you have to be different to impress them? Stop and rewind. Go back to the caterpillar that you were before you got your beautiful wings. Who loved you then? Who respected you then? Who saw the beauty within you then? Those people right there are the ones who deserve to be impressed by you. Not the ones who make you feel small even though you're way bigger. Not the ones who make you feel worthless even though you deserve to be sitting on a throne in a kingdom of your own.

Unjustified Excuses

There's absolutely nothing wrong with giving people excuses. It just goes to show how positive you are deep down, how able you are to see the good in people, and how able you are to see past the faces that they show. The real mistake is when you treat those people as if they've tried to express those excuses to you, as if they've put the effort forward to clarify their words or actions. The problem is when you make those excuses into apologies in your own head and forgive without being asked forgiveness or even being thought of as worthy of being asked for forgiveness. The problem is when you don't allow people to feel the need to make an effort to hold a spot in your life. If you're going to keep making them feel that you're okay no matter what they do, then don't wonder why they continue to do what they do. If you're willing to spend hours trying to justify their actions, what have you left to worry about your own?

You Are the Sun

For them to see you shine, you must stay far away, for you are just like the sun; when you're too close, your light makes them blind. And when you're too far, they seek you. So let them seek you. They're getting your light regardless, but appreciating your presence is different from recognizing your existence. If they don't appreciate your presence, they may never even recognize your absence.

Be Sought

Whatever you do, do it with purpose. Being focused is not something to be ashamed of. It is something to be proud of. When you know what you are doing and have a clear vision of where you are going, you will not need to chase opportunities. Opportunities will seek you. Happiness will chase you. And, instead of being a choice, you will be the one choosing.

I Deserve It

I'd rather be disappointed by the truth than satisfied with a lie. Respect me, not because I respect you but because I deserve your respect. How pleased would you be if you found out I respected you only because I wanted you to respect me back or because I wanted something in return? I respect you because you deserve it. Don't listen to me just because I listen to you. I listen to you because you deserve to be heard. Don't be nice to me just because I'm nice to you. I'm nice to you because you deserve to be treated right. Don't show me that you care just because you know I care. I care for you because your heart needs care. If your thoughts and feelings are not genuine, point them in a direction other than mine. If I only give you what you deserve, at least keep me away from what I don't deserve.

Because You Are a Good Heart

Here's the thing about people with good hearts. They give you excuses when you don't explain yourself. They accept apologies you don't give. They see the best in you when you don't need them to. At your worst, they lift you up, even if it means putting their priorities aside. The word *busy* does not exist in their dictionary. They make time, even when you don't. And you wonder why they're the most sensitive people. You wonder why they're the most caring people. You wonder why they are willing to give so much of themselves with no expectation in return. You wonder why their existence is not so essential to your well-being. It's because they don't make you work hard for the attention they give you. They accept the love they think they've earned, and you accept the love you think you're entitled to. Let me tell you something. Fear the day when a good heart gives up on you. Our skies don't become gray out of nowhere. Our sunshine does not allow the darkness to take over for no reason. A heart does not turn cold unless it's been treated with coldness for a while.

If You Ever Come Back, I Will Tell You:

The sun is closer to you
than I will ever be.
So burn,
if you wish.
You will not
see the shadow of me
even if you become
the sun
yourself.

I am not arrogant,
but you left a scar on my heart
that turns blue
every time I think of
you.

Know Thyself

After all of this,
I realize that you never really
knew me.
I never really knew me
either.

Don't base your self-worth
on the words of those who
don't even know the real you,
including you.

You don't have to be okay
with me
or with what I did with
what happened to me
for me to be okay
with myself.

Lose as many people as you need to
in order to not lose yourself.
No one worth keeping
in your life
is worth you
losing yourself.

CHAPTER 10

FINDING
HAPPINESS

Silver Lining

Have you ever been told not to show others your happiness or the good things that have come your way because they might envy you? Don't worry about those who cannot be happy for you, who cannot see the beauty within you. Beauty from within allows you to see goodness in others. It makes you see beauty in the simplest of things, to be content and to appreciate what you have before you ask for more, to value the moment you live in, and to hope for others in the same way that you hope for yourself. It allows you to forgive and forget at the same time that you learn. It allows you to be positive, to be optimistic, to see that silver lining even before you see the cloud. Everyone has this beauty, but it exists along with other characteristics, which may be in an imbalance at times: envy, hatred, pessimism, ungratefulness, discontent, jealousy, etc. Unfortunately, those characteristics will make others attribute your success and happiness to the things that you have, to the superficial things in your life, instead of looking and actually seeing the real you. People have a difficulty admitting that you are actually successful because of your hard work or because of your determination. They have a hard time admitting that you actually deserve the happiness that you have, so they are unable to be happy for you. You sometimes give those people a license to affect your feelings, and they use it against you, maybe not intentionally, but they do use it against you one way or another. You think that someone being rude, disappointing, or just plain weird around you is doing so because of something that you've done wrong. That right there is the beauty within you refusing to see that others may actually be responding to those negative characteristics within themselves. Hold on to that beauty within you, and let it prevail over other characteristics, because that is what keeps you moving forward while others are busy trying to figure out the *things* that make you happy.

Choose

Today, I choose to be happy. I choose to let go. I choose to be myself. To love myself. To cherish myself. Today, I choose to let go of the people whose company is toxic to my peace of mind. Today, I choose to be free. I choose to liberate my soul from the aches it's been through. Today, I choose to stay away from closed doors. I choose not to craft a wall around my heart. I choose to decorate it with the lessons I've learned. I choose to paint it with respect and confidence. Today, I choose to forgive myself. For being too much of myself. For allowing myself to hurt myself. Today, I choose to embrace my flaws. I choose to accept my mistakes. Today, I choose to change. I choose to be better. I choose to move forward. I choose to guard my soul. Today, I choose to be brave. I choose to say no when saying yes hurts. Today, I choose to be wise. I choose to walk away from places I don't belong. I choose to embrace my time. For all that is timeless is precious. All that is precious is unique. All that is unique is different. And all that is different is beautiful. Today, I choose to be beautiful.

Happiness Is in Your Hands

When people's definitions of happiness differ, the difficulty of reaching that happiness also differs. If happiness means money or status to you, then wait to pursue it, but if it means seeing and appreciating what you have, caring for your family, seeing beauty in the simplest things, then start now. While you are doing that, others will need something to keep them motivated to achieve their shallow goals of money or power. They will envy you for being so happy with so *little*. People may befriend you for an ulterior purpose, smiling back at you when you smile, not out of happiness for your happiness but out of questioning. How can you be so happy? How can they reach that happiness? How can they take that happiness away? That is what greed can do to people. Greed doesn't always have to do with money, and it is even worse when it has to do with happiness because people start building their happiness on the misery of others, and, oh, how hurtful and deceitful that can be. At the end of the day, be thankful for your health and family. Don't let any insignificant things or people get in the way of this aura of happiness that you choose to surround yourself with.

Simplicity Is the Key

We often fail to see the beauty in the simplest things in life: a smile, a fresh breeze of air, a full moon, a sky full of stars, a simple act of kindness, an inspirational conversation, a childhood memory, a mother's kiss. These are the things that make life beautiful because they will always be there as a reality or a living memory. These simple things do not have a price attached to them, unlike the things we strive for nowadays that we think will make us happy. When we fail to appreciate simplicity, we fail to see and appreciate the most beautiful and important things in our lives. When we fail to appreciate simplicity, we fail at being truly happy.

Happiness Perfected

There are moments when perfection stands in time and space, when the beauty of the moment does not need to be explained, because no words are strong enough. Those are the most beautiful moments in life. When the sunset meets the sea, when the raindrops meet the thirsty crusts of the earth, when the waves hug the shore, when the storm ends and the rainbow begins, when a baby smiles or holds your hand. When beauty meets modesty, when humbleness meets sincerity, when sadness meets empathy, when happiness meets genuineness. Those moments cannot be re-created. They cannot be equated with a price, and neither can happiness. So if you took your happiness from those moments, could you even try to put a price on it? Would you even try to get your happiness from things that are sold and bought? Would it even be possible for you to love people for what they have rather than for who they truly are?

A Moment In Between

Between all the rain and shadows, the clouds and darkness, the nights and their troubles, there are moments of sunshine that you must learn to cherish. Just like sadness doesn't last too long, those moments of happiness might not either. Put happiness in your heart when it comes your way as you would put sadness. You are not being selfish by doing that. You deserve to be happy. And moments of happiness come just like moments of sadness. Moments of sunshine come just like moments of rain. You can choose to bask in the sun, just as you choose to get drenched in the rain.

Wholeheartedness

Allow your eyes to speak
a story that
words cannot explain.
Allow your smile to sing
a beautiful melody
to the beats of your heart.
Allow your heart to beat to
the rhythm of a happiness
untold.
Allow your mind to sail
a thousand ships to the shore
of serenity.
Be brave.
Be happy.

I Will Tell You Again and Again

I hope that
your soul finds
peace
and that your heart
reaches
home.
I hope that
lights
light up your way
and that
happiness
takes over the
pains of
your yesterday.

*Set peace to the fire
in your soul.*

A Home for Pain

If pain built a home in
your heart,
remember that it has
doors.
And it has
windows.
Open the windows to
allow happiness in.
Better yet, open the doors and
walk outside.

Happiness is at your door,
desperately waiting for you to
open the door and
let it in.
Trust your heart and
open that door.

A Letter to Myself

Darling,
When did your heart become so weak?
When did the light in your eyes fade?
When did you disappear into the darkness?
When did you start believing that you were
nothing?
Did you forget the beauty that
once shined from your soul?
Did you forget to see yourself
through your eyes before you saw yourself
through theirs?
Did you forget that happiness comes from within
you?
Smile, darling.
You are beautiful.
You don't need them to look at you
before you look at yourself.
You don't need them to love you
before you love yourself.

You cannot change
a beginning
that began in the past.
You can end it
and start a new beginning
that begins now.

There is a heart inside of you
waiting to be loved by you.
Don't let it down.
Don't let yourself down.

CHAPTER II

GRATITUDE

Priorities

Hold on to those whom you love very tightly. Love them back, respect them, cherish every moment you spend with them, and make them smile. Do not let a stressful day get in the way of spending the right time the right way on the right people. It's a balance that you can and must strike to make every day worth living. Don't let the day come when you will regret not doing this. Life passes by as quickly as the sun sets and as quickly as the night turns into day. Don't let life pass you by. Fill it with the love that you have in your heart and it will bounce right back.

Reframe Gratitude

We always complain that we are given more than what we can handle. It's true. If we only knew what that truly meant, we would stop complaining and start showing more gratitude. Take a moment to be honest with yourself and think deeply. Reflect. Think of all of the things that you have. Are you handling them correctly? You are given a heart that has the capacity to love until no limit can be drawn, but, somehow, you build a tiny little wall around it to *protect* it. But what are you protecting it from? What keeps it beating? Your heart has the capacity to give because it wants to, not because it has to, but somehow you convince yourself to stop it from giving unless it must. It has the capacity to flutter with happiness over the simplest, most beautiful details of life: a child's smile, a mother's hug, a random act of kindness on the street, the determination in someone's eyes, a kind word, etc. Yet, somehow, you make it immune to seeing those things because you're so busy looking for bigger sources of happiness, not realizing that if you can't appreciate the little things, you can never appreciate the bigger ones. They may satisfy you temporarily, but they will never bring you true happiness simply because they don't last or your interest in them fades. You have a mind that has the capacity to be the most logical. It can talk you through any kind of problems that you have, yet you convince yourself that others can solve them for you better than you can. Your mind has the ability to put you first, yet you allow yourself to let others make you doubt yourself. Before you complain of being given more than what you can handle, think of everything that you already have that you take for granted. If you think that you've been given more than what you can handle, you must have been given more than what you deserve.

We Are in This Together

When you're going through a rough time, keep this in mind: Every person on earth has problems of his or her own, young or old, wealthy or poor, healthy or sick. You may look around and see happy faces. You may look around and see that everyone else's life is perfect because they have what they want or what you wish you had. Do you realize that that's how people look at you too? Do you realize that, to some people, you may seem like the happiest person on earth, with the most perfect life? You may be feeling like you're living in a blur. You may not care about how you interact with those around you because you're so engulfed in your own troubles. You may think that they don't even care about how you treat them because they're already happy. What difference is your smile or nice gesture going to make, right? Wrong. You may not be strong enough to draw a smile on your face when you're troubled, but others are. Their troubles may be bigger than yours, worse than yours, and more hurtful than yours. Just because they don't talk about them doesn't mean they don't exist. So, before you look at others and assume things about their lives, or judge them for doing the things that they do, think of how they could be looking at your life and thinking the same. Once you accept this fact, life becomes on your side. Happiness will seep through the broken pieces of your soul, and contentment will sew the pieces back together.

Moments to Live For

Think back to the moments when you felt that you'd made a difference in someone's life. Think back to the moments when you saw someone else's eyes light up because they saw the best in themselves through your eyes. Think back to the moments when your efforts to make someone realize what they are capable of doing finally started having an impact on them. Think back to the times when you felt that you were standing at the edge of a cliff, uncertain whether jumping would take you down to the lowest valley of disappointment or fly you up to the highest sky of happiness. Think back to the moments when happiness came so fast at you that you lost track of time, of space, of logic. Think back to the moments when you did something good for the sake of goodness without anyone knowing but yourself. Think back to the moments when you chose silence over words because words could not do justice to your thoughts, whether it was a happy or sad silence. Think back to the moments when your smile could not possibly contain your happiness, when your heart ceased to beat so fast. Think back to those moments and tell me, isn't your life truly worth living? Weren't those moments truly critical for making you who you are? Be thankful for those moments so that you don't become immune to them when they happen again and again, because they most definitely will. Whether you notice them or not is based on how much you've cherished them before.

Thank You for Silencing Me

Thank you for silencing me.
You led me to break
the silence of thousands who
have met humans like you
who chose not to use their hearts to love,
to allow their consciences to be just
or their broken pasts to heal
the wounds of the broken.
Thank you for loving me only when
you needed someone to love you.
You led me to understand
that in times of our need for love,
our hearts are the most beautiful.
Thank you for leaving me when
I needed you most.
You led me to myself.
You led me to needing my own heart.
You led me to my voice.

Don't you ever think that
I will hate you.
You taught me more than
any book
could ever teach me about
love,
life,
and authenticity with my feelings.

Just Because I Loved You

Just because I loved you,
and just because you hurt me,
I will not be ashamed to say that I loved you.
Because I really did love you.
I loved the loving person that
you were.
I do not love the cold person that you are now.
I loved the considerate person that
you were.
I do not love the inconsiderate person that you are now.
I loved the thoughtful person that
you were.
I do not love the deaf-hearted person that you are now.
You see, you once asked me what I loved about you.
And that is what I loved.
If you ask me today what I love about you,
I will tell you this:

I love the memory of the person that you
used to be.
I love that you allowed me to feel
the love that my heart can
contain.

I love the love that you showed me I can give.
I love the happiness that you showed me I could feel.
I love that you walked away.
I love that you did not stay.
I would have suffered if you stayed,
because of the person that you are
today.

I Am Courageous

I am going back again to
memories of you.
It makes me stronger
when I see how far
I've come
from you.

Crossroads

It took losing
you
to find
myself.
The day that
you walked away from
me,
I started taking
footsteps
toward myself.

Thank you
for putting me at the crossroads
between
finding myself and
making you want me.
I chose me.

Now That My Heart Is Broken

You broke my heart into
pieces.
Now that it's open,
I can see how much love
it has inside.
I can see how much love
every piece of it deserves,
and that's not the love that
you gave me.
So thank you for allowing
me to see
how much love
I have inside of me.

Even though your words
turned out to be
just words,
I thank you
for allowing me to feel
how much love my heart could give.
I thank you
for showing me
that my heart could survive
one more break.
Thank you.

You stayed a short while,
but
you made me want to write
about love,
not heartbreak,
again.
Thank you.

CHAPTER 12
LOVE

Love

I've never been in love, but I imagine it to be hard work. It is wanting for another person more than you want for yourself. It is giving without expecting the same in return. Once that expectation exists, problems are inevitable. It is having lots of arguments but never disrespect. Never humiliation, or even belittling. It's having someone who knows your weaknesses but who doesn't use them against you. Love is a sacred thing. It is by no means perfect, nor is it flawless. It is beautiful with every little imperfection in it. Perfection is always the same, but every imperfection makes each love a unique thing. Love is not a destination that we reach at one point. It is a journey that we already began the moment we were born. It is not something that you find but something you discover as you look more and more into your soul and learn more about yourself. It is having someone who makes you see the world in a better way. Someone who shifts your focus from the insignificant worries to the things that matter. Love never brings you down. It always lifts you up. It only grows. It is appreciating someone for who they are, not just for the way they make you feel. Love is seeing the beauty from within, for it is what lasts a lifetime. It is dedication to keep holding the hand of the one who loves you, even at heart. It is commitment to bettering oneself through the bettering of the other.

Unconditional Love?

Unconditional love is not true love. It's foolish love. True love has an unconditional willingness to listen and to understand. True love has an unconditional willingness to give, compromise, and sacrifice while working for one future, not two. It has conditions of respect. Don't tell me disrespect can come out of love. Don't tell me violence can come out of love. Don't tell me manipulation can come out of love. True love is not blind. It has a vision. Though it may not make sense who you love, how you love them should.

Together

Lucky you. I don't build walls. I build strong values that take me up higher. I work on my strength, my confidence, and my independence. So, do you need to work hard to get to me? Yes. Must you take the right steps to get up there? Definitely. You see, I don't want you to break down a wall I've built only to realize that I'm at the same level as everyone else you know. I also don't want you to climb a wall only to come down it on the other side. I want you to actually come up higher for yourself and for me so that we can both say that we've worked hard to build what we have, not worked hard to get to each other, because, once we do, what's next?

Respect Me

Own my heart with your respect. Free me from your deceit. Captivate me with your honesty. Rid me of your uncertainty. Challenge me with your thoughts. Enslave me with your genuineness. Impress me with your spontaneity. Treat me right, and I will treat you better. Keep me away from what I don't deserve, and I will bring you closer to what you deserve. Respect me. Be honest with me. I will give you nothing but multiples of that in return.

Care for My Soul

Your soul communicates with the people around you. It sends out signals in different ways, through your eyes, the way you talk, the way you walk, the way you move your hands, even the way you sit. Some people will pick up on those signals and interpret your feelings based on them, or they will not notice any difference. If they do, then they've got the key to your heart. If they don't, then they have much to learn about you. If you can look into my eyes and understand how I feel, then you've got the key to my heart. If you can know that the slightest change in my voice means that I am happy, sad, frustrated, amazed, irritated, or tired, then you are close to me because you are close to my soul and you can understand the way that it is expressing itself. Your soul can communicate with mine, understand mine, and care for mine. Therefore, I will care for yours.

A New Language

If my heart could speak, it would need a whole new language to express the way I feel. If my heart could create a piece of art, artists could not handle the power of its feelings. If my heart could sing, composers would not be able to put together its symphony, the softest ever made. If my heart could smile, it would flutter out of my chest and into my eyes to see the world with a touch of beauty and a hint of joy.

Through Their Eyes

See yourself through the eyes of those who love you. They see all of the goodness in you when you fail to see it. They see the best in you when you see the worst. They are always ready to lift you up even before you fall down. They see every reason why you deserve happiness, love, and joy when you may feel that you're the furthest from deserving all of that goodness. Learn to care about those who care about you before you try to make those who don't even notice you turn your way.

Tragedy

Don't think that your
departure carving a scar
into my soul
was the tragedy.

The tragedy of someone
leaving
has been the definition of
my life.

The true tragedy is that
you had the chance to be
different and
stay.

You are no different from
anyone who came before you.

If you wanted to be different,
you should have stayed.

The Bigger Tragedy

To choose to fall in love is
to choose to take
a risk.

To be hurt or
let go is
a tragedy.
And it is
possible.

But to choose
to not take the risk
and miss the chance of finding
the love of your life is
a bigger tragedy.

And it is also possible.

Letting You Go

I stopped choosing you when
I chose to
stop
choosing you.

You'll Know

I look back at the moment
I knew that I fell in love
with you.
I wanted to tell the world
what it felt like,
so I wrote:

"I never knew what they meant
when they said, 'you'll know,'
until
I knew.
And I never knew what they meant
when they said, 'time heals,'
until
I felt free."

Now I know
that I never really knew
and that I am free
not because I left you
but because I came back to
myself.

Astray

I asked you what I meant to you,
with my heart beating out of my chest.

I was afraid of losing you
if you did not pass this test.

I told you that I was tired
of reading between the lines.

I asked you to tell me
if you could see the spark in my eyes.
I told you that I was ready to walk away
and never speak to you after this day.

If you could just tell me
if *you* wanted *me* to stay.

You asked me what I wanted,
your honesty, confidence, loyalty, or perhaps more?

I told you that I wanted it all,
with some love and a spark in your eyes that I'd
forever
adore.

I told you that I wanted you
to try harder.

You promised me to do so,
but, oh, how I wish I were smarter.

Now I realize that when you ask for love,
it's not as true as when it comes your way.
And when the lines are blurred,
your search for love may have gone too far
astray.

I Once Felt This Way About You

Your love flies my soul to the moon.
It makes the sun revolve around my heart
and the stars dance in my eyes.

Your tenderness throws me in the ocean.
It plants pearls in my heart
and lifts me to the sky.

Your touch sends butterflies down my veins.
It makes roses grow in my heart
and sews my pains into traces of smoke.

Your strength cradles my heart to sleep.
It beats my heart to life
and breathes my soul to paradise.

The Whole World Is Mine

I once wrote you:
"I don't care if
the whole world
looks in a direction
opposite from mine.
If you look at me,
the whole world is mine."

You Choose

To you,
The tears that they
caused you
can be just tears or
rain that cleanses
the sorrows out of
your soul.
You choose.

The Surrender

A weakness within me has shattered the walls I've built within myself,
against myself.

I may have been successful at giving,
but I never know when to stop.

I worked so hard to break down others' walls that
I forgot to break down my own.

I worked so hard to understand others' silence,
but I forgot to understand my own.

I lifted, with every bit of me,
the weight off of so many people's shoulders and hearts,
but I forgot about my own burdens.

My bones have been bruised by the burdens I've accumulated.

My heart has been beating slower and slower.

My thoughts cannot bear the chaos in my mind.

So I decided to surrender.

I give up.

And if I were to hide my wings and bundle myself
back up into my cocoon, would you then try to take what I give,
understand my silence, or lift the weight off my shoulders?

Feeling like you will give up
does not mean that you
have to
give up.

Why do you want to love me?
I will traumatize you.

I hear your words
through my wounds.
I see your face
through my wounds.
I talk to you
through my wounds.
And I will love you
through my wounds,
just like your love will enter me
through my wounds.

I want to tell you
that I am falling for you,
but fear of this moment
stops me.
My heart reminds me:
Don't allow room
for shame.
Tell the people you love
that you love them.

Too Proud

I may be too proud to tell you how I feel or that I need your care. I may be too proud to express how much it means to me that you are doing well and that you are happy. I admit that I am too proud to admit that I have feelings. The thing is, people only see extremes. So, I would rather seem arrogant than needy, although I am not needy. I would rather seem strong than desperate, although I am not desperate. I just want to be content, so I don't want to ask for more. I just want to be happy. If I ask you to care, your care will only be a compliment. It will not be genuine. If I ask you to respect me, your respect will seem like a burden to you. If I ask you to love me, your love will be out of pity. I will keep my pride, and you continue to be blind. But you should know that life is always easier for the one who's loved because all he or she has to do is love back instead of fall in love with the unknown. Life is always easier for the one who is cared for because all he or she has to do is care back instead of care unconditionally. I made my decision to take a risk. Now you make yours.

Let Me Be Your Weakness

You are the weakness of those who love you. When they look at you, they see past your face. They feel greatness standing in front of them. They see happiness that they feel they don't deserve. They are willing to stand aside and see you shine rather than risk standing by your side, because they feel that they just might not give you the happiness that you deserve. Admire those who respect you even though they know how forgiving you'd be if they didn't. Those deserving of your love don't take advantage of your ability to forgive because they know how hard it is to forget. Admire those who are kind to you even though they know that you would make an excuse for them if they didn't. Those who love you don't take advantage of your innocence because they know how hard it is to maintain a pure heart in a dark world. I admire those who strengthen me even though they know my weaknesses. I admire those who acknowledge my presence even when I feel invisible, because those are the ones who will understand my silence when I feel that my words are choking on disappointment. I admire those who see me as different, but I love those who see me as unique.

Roses and Thorns

I want your roses with
your thorns.
Roses are tender.
They will soothe my heart.
Thorns are sharp.
They will teach me how
not to use
the thorns of my own.

What You Don't Need

You do not
need
what does not
want
you.

You should not
want
what does not
want
you.

*I beg you to keep
your soul
healthy.*

Before I Fell in Love, I Always Knew I Wanted This

I want you to love my heart
before you love my face,
love my vision
before you love my eyes,
love my wisdom
before you love the comfort that
my thoughts give you,
love my silence
before you love my words,
love my compassion
before you love how helpful I can be,
love the person that I am
before you love the person that
I want to be.
Respect me
before you love me.
I promise you no less than that
in return.

Now I know that saying this
is not enough.
The love that you accept
is the love that you will get.

Patience

Don't seek love
just to be in love.

Better wait years for the
right person
than wait years
for the right love
from the
wrong person.

Filling the Gaps

It is better to wait years
for the right love
than to stay in love
with someone who does not
love you
just so you can say that you are
in love.

Flashback

"You love too hard,"
he said.
"It's the only way to love,"
I replied.

I am tired of
every person coming my way
telling me that I am too
needy for love.
I am not needy
for love.
I just love.

No One Can Own Your Heart

It's a shame for you
that you chose not
to fight the wars
in my battlefield.
It's a shame for you
that you were a coward
and waved your white flag.
You surrendered.
What a shame.
The king who will own my heart
must be brave enough
to endure the chaos of purity within
me.

*Now I know that
no king can
own
my heart.
I am the owner of my own
empire.*

How do I tell you
not to compare me
to other women?
Not to love me more
because you love them less?
Because you love *her* less?

Love *me*
for who *I* am,
not who I'm *not.*
Love me because
you love
me.

I knew that our souls
were connected
when you told me:
"The sight of you
and the sound of your voice
stimulate my brain
more than
the touch of
all the women whose bodies
I have explored."

I've never wanted roses
to resist wilting
more than I do now.
That's how I know
that I want this love
to last.

"Look at me."
Three words that cause
an earthquake in my bones.

CHAPTER 13
HOPE

Never Doubt

You may doubt that the moonlight will always enlighten your way in the darkest of nights. You may doubt that the sun will always strike its rays through the gloomiest of clouds to brighten your days. You may doubt that a rainbow will come after every storm, or that a shining star of hope will always be there for you to wish upon. But never doubt that there are people out there who will be your light in the darkest of nights, who will brighten your every day, and who will open your eyes to the bright side of every situation. Never doubt that there are people out there whose wishes are not for things of their own but whose wishes are to make your wishes come true. Give your soul a chance at being happy by truly believing that those people exist. If you exist, then they do.

When You Lose Hope

Don't allow a few humans who shattered your belief in humanity make you believe that good humans don't exist. They do exist. And the biggest proof is that you exist. If you exist in this world, you'd better believe that there are people like you out there. So when you find them, be their friend, empower them, give them a voice, give them the care and love and kindness that you would give to everybody else out there in the world. But because you know how much you need it, being the good heart that you are, give it to them in abundance.

Better Places

There will always be places that don't welcome you, people who don't want you in their lives, and dreams that just don't work out. But that doesn't mean that there aren't other places that will welcome you. That doesn't mean that there aren't other people who would love to have you in their lives. And that doesn't mean that there aren't bigger dreams for you. Maybe you're meant to be in better places. Maybe you're meant to have better people in your life. Maybe you are meant to reach higher dreams than the ones that you have planned. So don't despair, trust in fate, and go for what you truly believe is the best thing for you or that puts your heart and soul at peace. And it will work out.

Moonless Nights

Even on moonless nights, the stars don't cease to shine. Even when the clouds conceal the sun in weary skies, every creature believes in its existence. Even when the thirsty bits of earth long for the slightest mist of water, they always accept the rain, no matter how long it takes. The branches of abandoned trees never reject to give rest to a restless bird. Even death springs new life in our hearts as it awakens our sleepless souls to the beauty of the life that we have and were complaining about. So tell me this. How can you be great if you expect to take more than you give? How can you expect to be different if you settle for being the same as everyone else? How can you lose hope after failing once? How can you tell your heart not to accept love after it's been hurt? Or your mind to cease to believe or trust after it's been deceived? How can you be afraid not to meet your fate at the right time, when fate is what chases you, not what you chase? The life you have ahead of you is a journey, and happiness is not a destination. Faith is in the heart, but it plants its seeds in your actions. If you work by your principles, you'll never make a decision that you'll later regret. No matter what fate it is you're chasing that you think is yours, none but what is meant for you will happen. Believe. Let the uniqueness of your heart overflow with hopeful patience that the happiness it deserves already exists and that, because of your uniqueness, it will come in a unique way.

My dear reader,

I hope that your soul
meets its fate
at the most beautiful,
pure,
and spontaneous
moment.

Don't Lose Hope

Someone,
somewhere,
is looking for the exact same love
that you have to offer.
The exact same love that
the one who hurt you did not appreciate.
Don't lose hope.
And don't settle.
The most beautiful love stories are those that
come after you realize what you deserve
and you actually finally get it.
You deserve someone who loves your
way of love.
Someone who loves you.

Even when it feels like the end,
it's not the end.

I must turn the page
and start anew.

I must start
a new story
about someone new.

The reason is coming.
Don't wait.
You'll slow down
its arrival
if you do.

WHAT'S NEXT

You made it. But we won't stop here.

Now pick up your pen and write down your story. It doesn't have to look like poetry. It doesn't have to sound poetic. It doesn't have to use words. Choose your way of expression and make a promise to yourself that whatever you create will come straight from your soul. Let it be as real as you feel that it is. Let it be as messy as it actually is. Let it be raw. Unfiltered. Not seeking to be validated by anyone but you.

Remember, you are the one walking this path. You are the one who went through what you went through. You are the one who felt every ache and stab. So stop waiting for someone to give you permission to heal in a certain way. Stop waiting for someone to show you the steps. Healing is a journey back to yourself. You know where to start. See yourself. Hear yourself. Understand yourself.

Start now.

ABOUT THE AUTHOR

Najwa Zebian is a Lebanese-Canadian activist, author, speaker, and educator. Her passion for language was evident from a young age, as she delved into Arabic poetry and novels. The search for a home—what Najwa describes as a place where the soul and heart feel at peace—was central to her early years. When she arrived in Canada at the age of sixteen, she felt unstable and adrift in an unfamiliar place. Nevertheless, she completed her education and went on to become a teacher as well as a doctoral candidate in educational leadership. Her first students, a group of young refugees, led her back to her original passion: writing. She began to heal her sixteen-year-old self by writing to heal her students.

Since self-publishing her first collection of poetry and prose in 2016, Najwa has become an inspiration to millions of people worldwide. She has become a trailblazing voice for women everywhere and was name-dropped by the *New York Times* and CBS News, among others. Najwa has also creatively collaborated with Google, RBC, Kohl's, and Cirque du Soleil. Drawing on her own experiences of displacement, discrimination, and abuse, Najwa uses her words to encourage others to build a home within themselves; to live, love, and create fearlessly.

@najwazebian

@najwazebian

@najwazebian

@najwazebian1

youtube.com/najwazebian

Andrews McMeel Publishing
a division of Andrews McMeel Universal
1130 Walnut Street, Kansas City, Missouri 64106

www.andrewsmcmeel.com

23 24 25 26 27 LAK 10 9 8 7 6 5 4

ISBN: 978-1-5248-6735-5

Library of Congress Control Number: 2021937775

ATTENTION: SCHOOLS AND BUSINESSES
Andrews McMeel books are available at quantity discounts with bulk purchase for educational, business, or sales promotional use. For information, please e-mail the Andrews McMeel Publishing Special Sales Department: sales@amuniversal.com.